ALLAMAH SAYYID MUHAMMAD HUSAYN TABATABA'I

Islam and the Contemporary Man

First published by al-Burāq 2014

Copyright © 2014 by Allamah Sayyid Muhammad Husayn Tabataba'i

All rights reserved. No part of this publication may be reproduced, stored or transmitted in any form or by any means, electronic, mechanical, photocopying, recording, scanning, or otherwise without written permission from the publisher. It is illegal to copy this book, post it to a website, or distribute it by any other means without permission.

First edition

Contents

Foreword	1
Chapter 1: The Way of the Primordial Human Nature [Fitrah]	4
Chapter 2: Some Philosophic and Scientic Problems	40
Chapter 3: Creation and Resurrection	102
Chapter 4: Miscellaneous Questions	117
Chapter 5: Human Origin and End	152
Chapter 6: Divine Knowledge Possessed By the Prophet and the...	164
Chapter 7: Refuting Wahhabi Contentions	173
Chapter 8: Essence and Existence	188
Chapter 9: Miscellaneous Questions	195
Chapter 10: Some Qur'anic Questions	219
Chapter 11: Some Objections and the Answers Thereto	225

Foreword

In the Name of Allah, the All-Beneficent, the All-Merciful

The invaluable legacy of the Household [*Ahl al-Bayt*] of the Prophet (may peace be upon them all), as preserved by their followers, is a comprehensive school of thought that embraces all branches of Islamic knowledge. This school has produced many brilliant scholars who have drawn inspiration from this rich and pure resource. It has given many scholars to the Muslim *ummah* who, following in the footsteps of Imams of the Prophet's Household ('a), have done their best to clear up the doubts raised by various creeds and currents within and without Muslim society and to answer their questions. Throughout the past centuries, they have given well-reasoned answers and clarifications concerning these questions and doubts.

To meet the responsibilities assigned to it, the Ahl al-Bayt World Assembly (ABWA) has embarked on a defense of the sanctity of the Islamic message and its verities, often obscured by the partisans of various sects and creeds as well as by currents hostile to Islam. The

Assembly follows in the footsteps of the *Ahl al-Bayt* ('a) and the disciples of their school of thought in its readiness to confront these challenges and tries to be on the frontline in consonance with the demands of every age.

The arguments contained in the works of the scholars belonging to the School of the *Ahl al-Bayt* ('a) are of unique significance. That is because they are based on genuine scholarship and appeal to reason, and avoid prejudice and bias. These arguments address scholars and thinkers in a manner that appeals to healthy minds and wholesome human nature.

To assist the seekers of truth, the Ahl al-Bayt World Assembly has endeavored to present a new phase of these arguments contained in the studies and translations of the works of contemporary Shi'ah writers and those who have embraced this sublime school of thought through divine blessing.

The Assembly is also engaged in edition and publication of the valuable works of leading Shi'ah scholars of earlier ages to assist the seekers of the truth in discovering the truths which the School of the Prophet's Household ('a) has offered to the entire world.

The Ahl al-Bayt World Assembly looks forward to benefit from the opinions of the readers and their suggestions and constructive criticism in this area. We also invite scholars, translators and other institutions to assist us in propagating the genuine Islamic teachings as preached by the Prophet Muhammad (s).

We beseech God, the Most High, to accept our humble efforts and to enable us to enhance them under the auspices of Imam al-Mahdi, His vicegerent on the earth (may Allah expedite his advent).

We express our gratitude to 'Allamah Tabataba'i, the author of the present book, and Mr. Dawud Sodagar, its translator. We also thank our colleagues who have participated in producing this work, especially the staff of the Translation Office.

Foreword

Cultural Affairs Department
The Ahl al-Bayt ('a) World Assembly

Chapter 1: The Way of the Primordial Human Nature [Fitrah]

Question

Is it reasonable to believe that Islam can manage the affairs of humankind and accommodate its needs despite the staggering improvements and advancements of the modern age? Shouldn't the modern human being, who anticipates traveling to the depths of the universe and conquering other galaxies by means of science, dispose of such antiquated religious beliefs in favor of a new way of life more befitting his achievements—a way of life that would enable him to concentrate the power of his mind and will more fully on adding to his praiseworthy achievements?

Answer

Before engaging in the answer to the above question, it should be noted that although we by nature cherish newness and prefer what is new over what is old, there are exceptions to this inclination. It cannot, for instance, be claimed that since "2 + 2 = 4" has been cited by people for thousands of years it is now outdated and must be dispensed with. Or, it would be absurd to contend that the social structure of human life, which has to date preserved the human species, is now too old and that from now on humans must live individually.

Obedience to civil law, which curtails individual freedoms to a great extent, cannot be abolished with the excuse that it is old and annoying. It would be unacceptable if someone claimed that since in the modern age the human being has embarked on conquering the universe by sailing out to new galaxies in spaceships, a new route must be pursued in human life that would free the individual from the burden of law, legislation, and governments.

The hollowness and absurdity of such assumptions are clear enough. The question of new and old is meaningful where there is room for evolution, where the object at issue allows of evolution and change—one day fresh and new but in time and after encountering the vicissitudes of life turning to frailty and decline. Thus, in discussions conducted for the purpose of shedding light on the truth (as opposed to vain polemics)—when debating natural phenomena, questions relating to the world of creation, and the laws of nature—such as the discussion at hand, poetic utterances of the fable of the new and the old have no place: "Every word behooves a certain place, every point a certain location."[1]

Let us now turn to our question: can Islam manage human society, considering the circumstances of the modern age? Of course, this question would seem superuous once the reality of Islam and the message of the Qur'an are understood.

For, Islam denotes the path to which human nature and cosmic order point. Islam conforms to the nature of the human being. As

---

[1] A Farsi proverb underlining the imprudence of making irrelevant remarks. [trans.]

such, it provides for and satisfies the true human needs, not the illusory desires or what one's sentiments dictate. Obviously, so long as the human being is what he is, his nature will remain the same. Regardless of the passing of time, the difference in habitat, and the varying circumstances, human beings share the same nature. This nature calls for a specific way of life, whether human beings be willing to pursue it or not.

In this light, the above question can thus be rephrased: would one attain to happiness and satisfy one's natural wishes, should he follow the path that human nature points to? This is similar to asking: would a tree reach its natural destination, should it grow in its natural manner with its needs provided for through its inherent natural structure? The answer to such a question is obvious.

Islam is the path of the primordial human nature. As such, it is always the correct path for the human being; it remains unchanged in the face of varying circumstances; it is the solution to our genuine needs.

It is the natural and inherent needs—not the sentimental wishes and delusional desires—that are one's true needs. It is the fulfillment of these inherent needs that begets felicity and happiness. In His Book, God says:

> "*So set your heart on the religion as a people of pure faith, the origination of God* [2] *according to which He originated mankind—there is no altering God's creation...*"[3]

Let us explicate—albeit briey—this subject. As is evident, each of the

---

[2] Please note that grammatically "the origination of God" is the appositive for "the religion". That is, the true religion is that which derives from God's creation; it is not a superimposed law. [trans.]

[3] Surah al-Rum 30:30.

multitudinous types of creatures that exist in the world of creation pursues a specific way of life and subsistence and follows a unique path to its individual destination.[4] Each creature can attain to felicity by traversing the path to its distinct destination and avoiding the obstacles that it may encounter. In other words, felicity is reached by navigating the path of life and avoiding the potential obstacles with the help of the innate apparatus with which every creature is equipped.

The grain of wheat, for instance, possesses a unique path. In its natural structure is embedded a specific mechanism, which is activated when the conducive circumstances are present. When activated, the inherent mechanism absorbs the necessary elements and nutrients in specific proportions needed for the growth and subsistence of the plant and consumes them so as to steer the plant toward its specific destination.

The wheat plant cannot alter the internal and external elements involved in its growth. It cannot, for instance, change its course, all of a sudden, to transform into an apple tree by growing a trunk, branches, and leaves and blossoming or turning into a sparrow, growing a beak and wings. This law holds true for all species, including the human being.

The human being, likewise, has a natural and inherent path for the pursuance of life, through which he may reach his destination, perfection, and felicity. Human nature is equipped with the special apparatus that can direct one on the natural and innate path to fulfilling one's true interests; God's Book affirms this:

"By the soul and Him who fashioned it, and inspired it with discernment between its virtues and vices: one who purifies

---

[4] The following verse attests to this truth: "Our Lord is He who gave everything its creation and then guided it." (Surah Ta Ha 20:50)

it is certainly felicitous, and one who betrays it certainly fails."[5]

Based on what has so far been said, it becomes clear that the true path of humanity leading to felicity is that which the primordial human nature guides to, that which secures the true interests of the humannbeing, in accordance with the requirements of the human constitution and the natural world, irrespective of whether we find it palatable or not, for it is the emotions that must follow the requirements of human nature, not vice versa. Thus, humankind should build its life upon the foundation of realism, not on the trembling columns of superstition and the delusional ideals feigned by human sentiment.

In this truth lies the distinction between Islamic law and other laws. The prevalent laws governing human societies follow the wishes of the majority (i.e., 51% of the population), whereas Islamic law conforms to the guidance of the primordial human nature, which reects the will of God, the Exalted. It is for this reason that the Noble Qur'an declares the enactment of laws as the prerogative of God:

"..Judgment belongs only to God..."[6]
"..But who is better than God in judgment for a people who have certainty."[7]

The legal systems that dominate secular societies are established either by the majority or by a dictator, regardless of whether they conform to the truth and fulfill the collective interests of human society. In the true Islamic society, however, it is the truth that rules; the wishes of

---

[5] Surah al-Shams 91:7-10.

[6] Surah Yusuf 12:40.

[7] Surah al-Ma'idah 5:50.

Chapter 1: The Way of the Primordial Human Nature [Fitrah]

the individuals defer to it.

Thus, the answer to another criticism—namely, that Islam is in conict with the natural trend of modern societies, that today's societies, which enjoy absolute freedom and satisfy their every desire, would not succumb to the numerous restrictions imposed by Islam—is also clarified.

Undoubtedly, in comparing the dark state of the modern human being—with depravation, wantonness, and oppression pervading all aspects of human life, threatening its very existence—with the luminous Islam, one would find absolute disharmony between the two. But when one compares the Divine primordial human nature with Islam—the primordial religion—one realizes their perfect harmony. Is it even conceivable that human nature should be at variance with the path it guides to? Unfortunately, however, corruption and illusion have defiled the primordial nature of the modern human being so that he no longer recognizes the path his nature inherently points to.

The rational solution to this predicament is to struggle to bring about the desirable state not to despair and succumb. Islam must come to the forefront and take the place of the other contending ideologies and worldviews. This will definitely be a strenuous process and would require much sacrifice.

History testifies that new methods and regimes invariably face fierce opposition from the status quo. They prevail only after winning innumerable battles—most of which are bloody. Still when they prevail, it takes time for effacing the name of the old opponent.

Democracy—which according to its advocates is the method of government most favorable to human needs—was established only after such bloody events as the French Revolution and similar incidents in other countries. Likewise, Communism (which according to its proponents is the synthesis of humanity's progressive efforts and history's most glorious blessing), in its edgling state, underwent much bloodletting that cost of millions of lives in Russia, Asia, Europe, and Latin America until it finally took root. In this light, the argument that people may find Islamic strictures unpalatable is not sufficient to prove Islam's incompatibility with modern society. Like the other systems, it would obviously need time to firmly establish itself.

Islam and the True Needs of Every Age

Without doubt, the importance and true value of a given scientific problem introduced for discussion and examination depends on the importance and value of the truth that is embedded within it and the results that it affects in its practical application and utilization in the ebb and ow of human life. A simple a matter as drinking water and consuming food is equal in value to human life, the most valuable blessing.

The notion of social life ingrained in the human mind, although a seemingly simple and mundane concept, is an invaluable one, for it is the cause of the magnificent world of humanity, in the context of which millions of actions interact every second to produce innumerable results, some of which are praiseworthy, appropriate, and beneficial while others are not.

It should go without saying, then, that the solutions provided in the pure faith of Islam to satisfy all the needs of people of all ages must be ranked most significant, for they are equal in value to the very existence of humankind, the greatest conceivable blessing. Any Muslim, aware of even the basics of Islam, would acknowledge this truth. This topic, however (like many other articles of faith established by Islam and ingrained in the minds of its adherents, being passed down quietly generation after generation), has not been duly explored, remaining buried in the believers' minds without being taken advantage of.

As far back as we, Easterners, can recount of the history of our ancestors, which goes back thousands of years, the dominant social institutions governing our affairs have never allowed us freedom of thought, especially in social matters.

The brief opportunity that was provided us in the beginning years of Islam and like the bright morning portended a promising future, did not last long. It was cut short by the dark incidents and turbulence fomented by a group of egotistic opportunists. Once again, we fell into captivity and slavery; once again we had to face the force of whips, swords, and the gallows and the solitude of prison cells—those infernal tortures and lethal environments—once again we were forced to revert to the ancient duty of "Yes Sir."

Under such circumstances, the best a believer could do was to retain his faith intact. As a matter of fact, that was exactly what the rulers and governors of the time favored so as to destroy the opportunity for free discussion. What they desired was that people occupy themselves with their own personal matters and not interfere with social issues.

Matters of society and politics were confined to the governments and the governors. The rulers had no fear of the people's innocuous conviction to the relatively simple matters of faith. Their concern was that people should not engage in free and inquisitive discussion, and for the accomplishment of this end they imposed themselves on the masses as the collective mind of the society.

For, they had correctly realized that the most effectual factor in social life was the individual will of the people controlled by their thoughts. So, by subduing the minds of the masses, the rulers fettered their wills. Hence, the statesmen's foremost concern was to control the minds of their people, which they did by placing themselves as the collective mind of the society. These are truths that anyone can verify beyond doubt by studying the annals of history with even the slightest attention.

And now European "liberty," after fully satiating the West, has turned to us Easterners in all its attractiveness. At first, it was portrayed as a dear guest. In time, however, it turned on its host, imposing itself as a stalwart landlord. Hailing liberty, Western imperialism uprooted the system that stied free thought—providing the best means and most favorable circumstances for reclaiming that lost treasure and forging a new life illumined by knowledge—but only to replace it as the new collective mind of the society.

At first, we failed to realize what was happening. When we did wake up from our slumber, we noticed that the days we had to yield to the orders of the old rulers were up—we no longer had to submit to the feudal lords, to the commands of the all-powerful masters, the "kings of all universe"—but instead we now had to live as our European benefactors instructed and follow the path they paved for us.

A thousand years have elapsed since Avicenna treaded this earth; his philosophic and medical books permeate our libraries and his thoughts our scholarly conversations—a blessing we have always taken for granted. We have been living for 700 years with the mathematic books of Khwajah Nasir al-Din al- Tusi before us. Our only acknowledgment of these great figures has been the recent conferences held in their 1000th and 700th anniversaries, and even in that we're mimicking European scholars.

The philosophic legacy of Mulla Sadra has been with us Iranians for the past 300 years, serving as a great source of illumination. The University of Tehran was founded many years ago. Philosophy has been taught there, with all the accouterments of academia, since its very beginning. Our philosophic heritage, however, has only received perfunctory treatment. But this suddenly changed a few years ago when a European orientalist speaking at a conference at Tehran University praised Mulla Sadra and his school of philosophy. His acknowledgement brought unprecedented interest to the study of Mulla Sadra's personality and philosophy.

These and other similar instances serve to illustrate our social and global status, shedding light on the debased state of the intellectual identity of our learned men. Those, on the other hand, who have succeeded in retaining a certain degree of intellectual independence, securing some of their intellectual heritage from being lost altogether, are gripped by a dual personality: they are infatuated with Western concepts but are also fond of their own Eastern heritage.

They try in vain to force a marriage between these two mutually exclusive cultures. One certain learned writer struggles to apply Islam to the concept of democracy in his book: "Islamic Democracy"; another, under such titles as "Islamic Communism" and "Islamic Socialism," construes Islam in the light of Communism and the abolition of class differences.

What a strange story. If Islamic realism is truly manifested only when it conforms itself to democracy or Communism (which have walked into our lives with their most captivating attractions), why should we not just dispose of Islam and spare ourselves the trouble of reconciling a bunch of outdated concepts from 1400 years ago with these "lively" concepts? However, if Islam is possessed of a distinct and independent identity—which it is—and offers a living and valuable truth, then what need is there to shroud its Divine beauty in a borrowed garment and advertise it in a false appearance?

In recent years—particularly, since the close of World War II—Western scholars have enthusiastically engaged in discussions and examinations regarding religion, publishing their studies at an ever- increasing rate. When taking on a problem, the curious scholar first attempts to construe it in accordance with the principles he adheres to. Then, he passes judgment as to the solution of the problem. In this light, Western scholars view religion as a merely social phenomenon that is the product, as is the case regarding society itself, of certain natural factors.

All religions, including Islam, from the point of view of Western scholars—those of them who hold an optimistic view of religion—are the fruits of the minds of geniuses who by purity of soul, profundity of insight, and an indomitable will succeed in formulating regulations for the purpose of reforming the values and behavior of their societies, thereby guiding them in the path to felicity.

These regulations, then, evolve in the course of the gradual progress of societies. Empirical evidence confirms, they contend, that human civilization is gradually navigating toward perfection, every day taking a fresh step toward progress.

This conclusion is corroborated by psychological, legal, social, and even philosophic arguments, especially in reference to dialectical materialism, which asserts that societies do not remain stagnant, and that, consequently, social regulations must of necessity change. Regulations those were able to secure the happiness of prehistoric human beings, who subsisted on fruit they plucked from trees and resided in caves, cannot satisfy the innumerous needs of modern society. The age of nuclear warheads cannot be governed according to regulations of the days when weaponry consisted of clubs and axes.

The regulations of the days when horses and donkeys were the sole means of transportation are no longer effective in an age when jets and nuclear submarines are means of transportation. In one word, the modern age does not—and should not be expected to—yield to the regulations of previous ages. The binding regulations of human societies are inevitably subject to constant alteration in conforming to the developments of human society. Alteration of laws governing social conduct in turn leads to change of values, for values are nothing more than habits and ingrained psychological states, which result from repeated practice.

The simple life of ancient times did not call for the sensitive measures required to steer life in the tortuous course of modern age. How could

Chapter 1: The Way of the Primordial Human Nature [Fitrah]

the social women of today practice the chastity of the women of ancient times?

The laborer and farmer of today's oppressed classes should not be expected to show the tolerance that was so characteristic of the oppressed classes of ancient times. Such threats as solar and lunar eclipses are no longer effective: the revolutionary minds that have conquered the outer space cannot be intimidated into believing such superstitions as trust in God and submission to His will. These examples illustrate, the proponents of this point of view claim, how societies of every age require regulations and morals appropriate to the ambiance of that particular age.

In line with that sense of imitation and submission present in Eastern intellectual circles, as mentioned above, Muslim thinkers have followed in the footsteps of their Western peers by applying the same curiosity to questions relating to the sacred religion of Islam.

The "enlightened" Muslim thinker contends that Islam is in essence the body of regulations that most effectively guarantees the felicity of human society. As such, the manifestations of Islam vary depending on the circumstances of each age. The way of life preached by Prophet Muhammad was only one of these manifestations. In this light, Islam applies to the most effective and godly regulations conducive to human felicity in each age. This is how the Westernized modern thinker interprets Islam's timelessness based on the "definitive scientific" criteria he boasts of.

But now let us turn to the Noble Qur'an—the heavenly book of Islam and the best speaker for this pure faith—to see what it has to say on this question. Does it concur with the above point of view or does it set forth certain doctrines, moral principles, and regulations as immutable and require humankind to follow them?

If the latter is correct, how does it solve the dilemma of being applicable to the ever-changing needs of various ages? Does Islam promote stasis in human society, shutting the door on the progress of civilizations and putting a stop to the progressive human activity? How can Islam refuse to conform to the inherent ux of the natural order, to which the human society is no exception?

The indubitable truth is that the Noble Qur'an, with its profound language, expounds religious concepts—Islam's derivation from the Unseen and relation with the order of creation and the visible and changing world, the mutability and immutability of religious doctrines, human virtues, and individual and social felicity—in a manner that is fundamentally different from the Western mentality. The Noble Qur'an views these subjects from a perspective that is beyond the purview of materialistic examination.

The Qur'an describes Islam as the set of doctrines and regulations to which the order of creation and specifically the evolving and progressive nature of the human being—as a member of the natural world which is in constant ux—guide. In other words, Islam, according to the Qur'anic depiction, comprises a set of regulations that are necessary requirements of the order of creation. Like their source [i.e., the order of creation], the regulations of Islamic law [shari'ah] are immutable, not subject to human caprice.

Islam is the embodiment of truth; it does not change to appease the whims of tyrants (as is the case in authoritarian states) or to satisfy the wishes of the majority (as is the case in socialistic and democratic states). Its regulations follow solely the decrees of the order of creation, that is, the will of God.

In what way does Islam provide for the needs of every age?

In discussions on the subject of society, it has time and again been reiterated that the human being, due to the critical needs that surround him and which he cannot individually satisfy, has no choice but to choose social life, thus becoming inured to a social existence. Moreover, in discussions of jurisprudence, as we may have all heard many times, it is elaborated that a society, in order to satisfy the critical needs of the individuals, must be governed by a set of regulations appropriate to the needs of the individuals, by means of which each individual could protect his veritable rights, enjoy the benefits of social life, and profit from the fruits of social interaction.

As can be deduced from the above two points, the principal and prime factor in instituting laws for a society is the fulfillment of the critical human needs, without which life would not endure. The direct result of forming a society and implementing the established regulations therein is the fulfillment of the critical human needs.

As such, the term *society* cannot correctly be applied to a crowd of people who have no meaningful interaction. Furthermore, regulations whose formulation or implementation does not positively affect the fulfillment of people's needs and the procurement of their happiness and felicity are not true regulations; a regulation is that which fulfills the needs and protects the rights of the people.

The presence of regulations which, at least partially and imperfectly, fulfill a society's needs and are generally consented to by the individuals is inevitable, even in the most uncivilized and primitive of societies. However, in uncivilized societies regulations are maintained in the form of tribal habits and customs, which are the outcome of desultory interactions materialized over a period of time or of the coercion of the more powerful elements of the society.

Even in our age, there are tribal communities in various corners of the globe that continue to prosper by maintaining their habits and customs. There must, nevertheless, exist regulations, conformed to by all or most individuals, to serve as the foundation for the society. In a civilized society, if it be religious, Divine Dispensation would rule, but if not religious, it would be governed in accordance with regulations born of the majority will, whether directly or indirectly. The main point, however, is that there cannot be a society whose people are not bound by a set of duties and regulations.

The Means for Determining the Social and Human Needs of the Individual

Now that it has been clarified that the principal factor in the formulation of regulations is the fulfillment of the needs of the individuals in a society, we must turn to other related questions: how may one determine the individual's social and human needs (of course they must be, whether immediately or not, recognizable at least to some extent)? Could the human being err in determining his individual and social duties, or is whatever he determines conducive to his felicity and should be endorsed without hesitation (which is to say that one's desires are sufficient to legitimize the obligations they point to)?

The majority of the "modern world" acknowledges the will of the populace as the source of law. However, due to the fact that the concurrence of the entirety of a nation's population on an issue is either impossible or very rare compared to the areas where they disagree, the will of the absolute majority—51 percent—is granted legitimacy and that of the minority—49 percent—is rejected, thereby depriving the minority of its liberty.

Without doubt, there is a direct relation between a population's

Chapter 1: The Way of the Primordial Human Nature [Fitrah]

wishes and their living circumstances. An afuent man, who has procured all the necessities of life, fancies plans that would never occur to someone destitute. If starving, one would crave for any type of food, whether delicious or not, without the least concern for scruples (such as if it belonged to someone else); but when satiated, he only reaches out for the most delicious of foods.

In times of comfort, the human being cherishes thoughts he would never consider in times of distress. Based on this reality, the evolution of human society, satisfying many of the older needs and replacing them with newer ones, has rendered certain ancient regulations irrelevant, prompting the human society to replace them with new laws or to modify them.

Hence, in thriving nations, old laws and regulations are constantly replaced with new ones. The reason for this process, as mentioned above, is that the basis of a people's laws is the collective will of the majority; it is this element that gives credibility to the laws and regulations of a nation (even if it be at odds with what is truly in the interests of that nation).

Nevertheless, we should consider with greater attention the fundamental factor responsible for the development of social laws: does social progress bring change to all spheres of human concern? Are there not common qualities shared by all societies of all ages? Does human nature (which is necessarily the basis of a portion of human needs, even as some other needs depend upon varying circumstances, situations, and environments) evolve? Aren't the body parts and organs we have the same as the first humans', with the same functions?

Were war and peace different from what they are now—killing human beings and the stop to such bloodshed? Did intoxication feel any different in Jamshid's [8] time? Was the pleasure of listening to

---

[8] In Persian mythology, the inventor of wine. [trans.]

the music of Nakisa and Barbad[9] fundamentally different from the pleasure that today's music produces? Did the natural structure of the ancient human being differ from today's human being? Did the internal and external functions and reactions of the ancient human being differ in any way from those of the modern human being?

Of course, the answer to all the above questions is clear. It would not be plausible to claim that humanness has gradually disappeared, being replaced by something else. Nor is it plausible to hold that the essence of humanity has faded and been replaced by a different essence. It would be equally implausible to argue that human nature, that which all human beings—black and white, old and young, intelligent and ignorant, of the Polar Regions and the tropical regions, of the past, present and future—share in common, does not require common needs or that human beings do not wish to satisfy those essential needs.

Such essential needs do exist, and they necessitate a set of immutable regulations, not subject to change of any type. When faced with an enemy that threatens their very existence, nations of all ages would unquestionably embrace war, if possible, as a means of defense, and if such an enemy would not be repelled except by bloodletting, they would consider it justified to employ such an extreme measure. No society may legitimately prohibit consumption of food, for it is one of the life-sustaining factors; nor may it prevent the satisfaction of sexual desire. There are numerous examples of such cases that require immutable regulations.

The above explanation clarifies the following points:

- The principal factor responsible for the existence of social laws and regulations is the satisfaction of the individuals' needs.
- All nations, including the primitive ones, follow laws and regula-

---

[9] Two pre-Islamic musicians who ourished during the Sassanid Dynasty. [trans.]

tions they have established.
- The criterion for determining the true needs of life, according to the modern world, is the will of the majority.
- The will of the majority does not always concur with reality.
- A portion of human laws and regulations change with the passing of time and in the course of social progress. These are the ones related to specific circumstances. However, there are also other human laws and regulations that pertain to the essence of humanity, which is shared in common by all human beings of all ages, irrespective of the varying circumstances and environments.

Let us now see what the Islamic viewpoint is in this regard.

The Basis of Islamic Doctrine

Islam is a universal and timeless religion. It aims, in its distinct educational program, at the "natural human being" that is, the object of its laws is simply the human being, irrespective of all distinctions. It embraces Arab and non-Arab, white and black, poor and wealthy, strong and weak, man and woman, young and old, knowledgeable and ignorant alike. The natural human being is he who has retained the Divine primordial nature, whose mind and will are pure and unsullied by falsehood and superstition.

There is no room for doubt in that the distinctive feature of the human being is his equipment with intellect and the faculty of contemplation, a Divine blessing of which other animals are deprived. The intelligence and will of all animals (excepting the human being), which control animal activity, are subject to their instincts. It is the provocation of those instincts that propels the animal to make a decision and to take an action. With this instinctual system, they proceed with their life-sustaining activities, seeking water, food, and other necessities of life.

The human being is the only animal that along with his various instincts and emotions—affection and antipathy, friendship and animosity, fear and hope, and all the other emotions of attraction and repulsion—is endowed with a judgmental mechanism responsible for reviewing the conicting demands of his emotions and faculties, judging what is truly in his interests. In some cases, it judges against a certain action despite the strong appeal of the emotions; at other times, it deems the action necessary, though it be repulsive to the emotions; and in cases where the true interests of the individual agree with his emotions, it gives its consent.

Based on the reality of human nature and the fact that the education and training of any species consists in cultivating the respective distinctions and peculiarities of that species, Islam has founded its educational program on intellection not sentiment. In this vein, Islam invites humanity to a body of pure doctrines, virtues, and practical laws, which the untainted and divine human nature would verify and vindicate of any possibility of falsehood and superstition.

The Cognitions of the Natural Human Being

In the purity of his nature, the natural human being comprehends that the vast cosmos—its tiniest particles as well as its most gargantuan galaxies, which journey toward the Unique God by the amazing cosmic order with the most accurate rules and numberless activities—is His handiwork. The natural human being understands that the multifarious parts of the cosmos together form a boundless unit, whose parts are intricately interconnected and bound by a perfect cohesion.

The various parts of the cosmos went hand in hand in order to bring forth the world of the human being—this small part of the cosmic body, an insignificant drop in the shoreless ocean of existence. The human being is the creation of the entire cosmos, the will of God. As a child of the world of creation, trained under its guidance, he has been fashioned into the human form—equipped with various internal and external faculties—through the operation of innumerable elements. His various faculties, emotions, intellect, and will constitute the apparatus by which the order of creation guides him to true felicity.

It is true that the faculties of intellect and free will enable the human being to distinguish good from evil, benefit from harm, thus being a free agent. Nevertheless, it must be borne in mind that it is the order of creation—the will of God—that has furnished his inward and outward with the faculties that render him a free agent.

Using the intellect with which he has been endowed, the natural human being realizes beyond doubt that felicity—his true goal in life—can be achieved only by attaining to the end that the order of creation has determined for him and toward which it guides him by means of the various faculties it has equipped him with. That end is what the Unique God, the Creator, the Trainer of the human being and the universe, has willed.

On these premises, the natural human being, then, resolves that the only path to felicity is to constantly monitor his existential orientation; reminding himself that he is an inseparable part of the order of creation and is governed by it, that he has been created by God, and as such must, by reading the book of creation, decipher his duties vis-à-vis the various situations he encounters. The content of this book, put in a nutshell, is that one must not demean himself except before the Unique God and that the demands of one's emotions and one's needs, when approved by the intellect, must be met.

Mutable and Immutable Regulations

The demands and needs of the human being are commonly incorporated into bodies of law. Such laws can be distinguished into two categories. One category comprises those laws which guarantee the wellbeing of the human being; that is, those laws which pertain to him as a human being living a social life, regardless of such peculiarities as the particular time and place he occupies. They include the set of doctrines and regulations that shape the relationship of humility and servility between the human being and his Lord (who is beyond change) and the general principles of human life regarding the need for food, shelter, marriage, and defense of one's right to life and social participation.

The second category of laws is those that are transient, regional, or delimited in some way by particular qualifications, thus being liable to alteration. Social progress, urbanization, alterations in the forms of societies, and the dissolution of old ways are among the factors that may lead to change in laws of this type.

For instance, the days when people traveled on foot, on horseback, or on other draft animals, rudimentary roads were sufficient, but with the development of the new bafing means of transportation, thousands of ground, maritime, and aerial regulations are required to secure safe transportation.

The primitive human being would satisfy his needs for food, clothing, shelter, and sex in ways which his primitive means allowed and which called only for the simplest of regulations, spending most of his time in trivial toils. Today, he pursues life with a bewildering speed, but due to the sophistication of vocations, every aspect of life has developed a technical sphere, demanding specialized fields of knowledge accompanied by thousands of complicating regulations.

Islam, which aims at the primordial nature of the human being, guides humanity to the unadulterated natural society, the unadulterated natural doctrines, the unadulterated natural practices, and finally the unadulterated natural destination. The pure intellectual conceptions of the natural human being in doctrine and action constitute the plan that Islam offers for humankind.

> *In this light, Islamic regulations are of two types: mutable and immutable. The latter—consisting of those regulations based on human nature and his essential qualities—is referred to as the shari'ah (Divine dispensation), the avenue to human felicity:* **"So set your heart on the religion as a people of pure faith, the origination of God according to which He originated mankind; there is no altering God's creation; that is the upright religion..."**[10]

The mutable regulations, which may change due to varying circumstances of time and place, are left to the discretion of the Prophet, his successors, and those whom they appoint. These authorities may alter the mutable regulations in light of the immutable principles and in response to the differing circumstances of time and place. These regulations are not technically considered part of the *shari'ah*:

> **"O you who have faith! Obey God and obey the Apostle and those vested with authority among you..."**[11]

This is, in summary, Islam's solution to the varying needs of different ages. However, the topic calls for a more thorough examination, which we will subsequently take up.

---

[10] Surah al-Rum 30:30.

[11] Surah al-Nisa' 4:59.

The Mutable and Immutable Regulations of Islam

In previous chapters, we learned that Islamic law distinguishes between two types of regulations: immutable and mutable. We will now elaborate further on this topic.

Immutable Regulations

The immutable regulations are those that have been established on the basis of the reality of human nature, which subsumes the urban as well as the rural, the white as well as the black, the strong as well as the weak, and individuals of all times and places. As soon as two or more individuals come together in a community, pledging to cooperate and support one another, they will inevitably encounter certain needs, which they have to endeavor to fulfill.

As the essence of their human constitution is identical, being endowed with similar inward and outward faculties, undoubtedly their needs will be of the same nature and as such would require a consistent set of regulations.

All human beings share the same intellectual cognitions. Rational judgment, unhampered by illusion and superstition, would generate identical conclusions in every individual. The cognitive faculties of all human beings alike achieve satisfaction through judgment and belief. Likewise, the various emotions—affection and antipathy, hope and fear—and instincts—sexual desire, the inclination to dress, to take shelter, etc.—are common to all human beings, and thus their dictates in all individuals must be treated similarly.

Due to the common human nature, it would be unreasonable to claim that satisfaction of hunger should be permissible in respect to one individual but impermissible in respect to another, or that one individual should heed the demands of his conscience but another should ignore them.

It would be equally absurd (bearing in mind the common human nature which has endured with the same faculties, emotions, and intellect for millennia) to assume that some ages require that the human being be persuaded by those truths which he deems self-evident whereas other ages require that he disavow them; that in some eras he should lead a social life but in other eras he should live in isolation; that at times he should defend his sacred beliefs but at other times he should relinquish his very existence to the enemy; that during some periods he should pursue a vocation in order to provide for his life whereas in other periods he should remain idle and jobless. These examples should suffice to illustrate that the natural human being, regardless of the changing times, requires certain immutable regulations.

This is exactly what Islam directs to in its primordial invitation. It proclaims that only the immutable regulations that derive from the order of creation, in general, and human nature, in particular, can guarantee human prosperity. Islam exhorts humankind to heed their Divine intelligence and conscience; to refrain from licentiousness, foolishness, and wantonness; and to abide by those principles they deem right.

To label submission to truths as blind imitation is wrong just as it is wrong to invoke the pretense of "national pride" or "custom" to stubbornly adhere to the ways of our ancestors. To attack theism as outdated while bowing to lustful rulers is not progress.

Islam literally signifies the exclusive worship of God, the Creator of the awesome order of creation, in line with the true human nature; it is this truth that it invites humanity to embrace. It is in this vein that Islam offers a set of doctrines, morals, and practices to humankind, declaring them truths that must be obeyed, as they constitute the primordial, unchanging, and heavenly religion. Islam presents its system of doctrine, morality, and practical law as a coherent unit in harmony with the system of creation. Of course, the limitations of this work do not allow us to elaborate on this system. We mainly intend to affirm that Islam incorporates a set of immutable regulations.

Mutable Regulations

In addition to the immutable regulations, which correspond to the immutable and natural needs of the human being, human society requires a set of changeable and mutable regulations, without which it would disintegrate. The reason for this is clear; despite the human being's immutable nature, the passing of time and regional discrepancies confront him with changing circumstances to which he must adjust.

These varying circumstances call for disparate regulations. In response to the need for such transient regulations there exists in Islamic law a principle to which we will in this discussion refer as the 'authority of the ruler', which accommodates the differing needs of people of various times and regions without nullifying the immutable laws of Islam.

Further Elaboration

In an Islamic society, religious law confers certain rights and freedoms on the individual in the framework of which he can conduct his affairs in the family domain as he wishes (of course, observing Islamic law). He may spend his money to the extent he deems prudent in providing the best foods, apparel, and furnishings for his family, or he may decide to the contrary; in the event of an incursion on his rights, he may legitimately decide to defend his dignity, or, as expedience should dictate, to concede and compromise on some of his rights; he may work day and night to accumulate wealth, or he may decide to cease work so as to attend to other duties.

The powers invested in the Muslim ruler (appointed according to Islamic law to yield general authority and to function as the intellectual fountainhead and the center of the collective thought and will of the Muslim society) for governing the Islamic state are similar in nature to those of the individual in the family domain.

Observing piety and the immutable laws, the Muslim ruler is authorized to establish regulations for managing the affairs of the Muslim society (e.g., maintaining order on roads, in residential neighborhoods, in the marketplace regarding business transactions, and in the interaction of the different entities within the society). In case of an attack, he may order the army to defend the Islamic state (having prepared the army with the necessary equipment and armaments), or to withhold retaliation and settle for a ceasefire, in accordance with what he finds expedient.

In facilitating progress in the fields of spirituality and public welfare, he may enact certain measures to accomplish major reforms. He may promote certain fields of knowledge and downplay others in accordance with the interests of the Islamic state. In other words, the Muslim ruler is empowered to enact any regulation conducive to the progress of the Islamic society and in the interests of Islam and the Muslim nation. There are no legal limitations to his power to enact and enforce such regulations [other than the immutable Islamic law and morals].

Although such regulations are binding according to Islamic law and the Muslim ruler—whom Muslims are obliged to obey—is duty-bound to enforce them, they are not considered part of the *shari'ah* (the Divine Dispensation). The legality of such regulations is naturally contingent on the particular circumstances that necessitate them, and hence as soon as the circumstances change, the regulations would expire, at which time the Muslim ruler must inform the public of the expiration and set forth new regulations to accommodate the new circumstances. However, unlike the regulations enacted by the Muslim ruler, the contents of the *shari'ah* are eternal and immutable. No one, including the Muslim ruler, has the authority to alter or annul them.

Clarifying a Misconception

The summary explanation provided above should suffice to prove the invalidity of the criticism leveled against Islam in this regard. Those who claim that social life has so greatly evolved that there are no common qualities that today's societies and those of 14 centuries ago share in; that modern life necessitates numberless regulations which were unimaginable to the people of the early Islamic era (just the regulations pertaining to the transportation sector of today's societies are far greater than all the regulations of Prophet's time put together); that because Islamic law does not include such regulations it is not fit to govern modern societies—those who make such arguments lack an accurate understanding of Islam and its mutable regulations. They presume that Islam only incorporates a set of rigid and inexible regulations and that consequently the only way Islam could ourish would be by Muslims' wielding swords and obstructing the progress of human civilization—such ignorance.

Another group of critics, on the other hand, contend that the inevitable evolution of social life will, no doubt, result in the gradual alteration of all social regulations. Hence, the immutable Islamic law, if ever valid, was only relevant to the Prophet's era, with its peculiar circumstances and thus is not indefinitely applicable.

These detractors have not paid sufficient attention to jurisprudential discussions, hence missing the fact that all civil laws prevalent in the various countries around the globe include certain unalterable elements. Without doubt, the laws of modern times are not entirely different from those of ancient times and those of future ages. There are certain common elements which passing of time never outdates (some examples were provided above).

Islam's methodology in establishing regulations (including both the immutable Divine law, which derives from the wellspring of Revelation, and the mutable regulations that are based on the 'authority of the ruler', in accordance with which regulations are enacted through council and enforced by the Muslim ruler), although founded on rationality and not on the capricious wishes of the majority, is to some extent similar to modern states.

Most modern states have a constitution, the alteration of which is beyond the authority of their governments and even parliaments. Their laws, however, also incorporate other regulations that are enacted mainly by the parliaments and occasionally by the governments; the latter are susceptible to alteration in the course of a country's development.

To expect Divine Dispensation to include the particulars relating to the believers' lives is similar to the expectation that state constitutions should incorporate the details regarding traffic regulations. The incorporation of such minute details would subject them to the need for frequent revision, an unreasonable measure (this is in reference to the first criticism, which assumes that Islamic law is a set of inexible regulations whose date of expiration has passed).

Furthermore, the detractors' criticism that the *shari'ah* (Divine Dispensation), which resembles a constitution in the framework of Islamic law, should be open to alteration is unacceptable for the same reason that a modern state's constitution (which outlines the fundamental issues, such as the country's independence, the need for a president, and the like) may not be altered (this is in reference to the second criticism). Thus, both the first criticism and the second one are ill-founded.

There is, however, one other question (an offshoot of the second criticism) that merits mention: It is true that there are legal elements not prone to change, however, this does not in itself prove that the regulations of the *shari'ah* can guarantee the felicity of humankind for all time. Can modern civilization continue its progress with such rituals as the canonical prayer, fast, *hajj*, *zakat*[12], and the like? Can Islamic regulations concerning slavery, women, marriage, commerce, usury, etc., continue to be relevant in the modern world? These and other related questions call for extensive discussions.

The Question of the Termination of Prophethood

Question

What would be the appropriate reply if someone claimed that the Prophet's declaration that he was the last in the line of Divine prophets means that humanity's need to be guided by the wisdom that transcends human intelligence has been fully satisfied by the Greek, Roman, Christian, and Islamic civilizations, by the Torah, the Bible, and the Qur'an. The Prophet's term was the inauguration of a new age in which, building on the Divine heritage of God's prophets, humanity can continue life and advance toward perfection without the help of new revelation from God, hence the termination of prophethood?

Those who are of this persuasion maintain that humankind have achieved the sufficient level of intelligence to be able to manage their affairs, establish peace, and pursue their felicity on their own. Human beings are self-sufficient now, mature enough to endure without Divine guidance. Human intelligence has now superseded Divine revelation. What should be our stance vis-à-vis such a conception?

---

[12] A certain religious tax. [trans.]

Answer

Let us first rephrase the above argument in order to better understand it. The human being, like all other creatures, is traversing the path to perfection. The passing of time and the evolving existential states effect in the human society new circumstances accompanied by an increased need for new modes of guidance.

Each new phase of human progress demands a new way of life, a new set of obligations and regulations appropriate to the special guidance needed for that particular phase. In this light, no religion or way of life may legitimately be considered eternal, the *shari'ah* of Islam being no exception. Therefore, when the Prophet announced that he was the "Seal of the Prophets" [*khatam al-nabiyyin*], he meant, these "modernists" contend, that up to his time, due to the deficiency of human intelligence, humankind was in need to be guided by Divine wisdom, which transcends human intelligence.

However, humanity's maturation facilitated by the advent of Greek, Roman, and Islamic civilizations and the revelation of the Divine books—Torah, Bible, Qur'an—(i.e., supra-human guidance) has elevated them to a new intellectual height, liberating them from the need for revelatory guidance and enabling them to stand on their own feet. This is the essence of the argument in question.

There are several aws in this argument. First, although it is true that both the human individual and the human society are advancing toward perfection, nevertheless, the scope of human perfection is finite in terms of both quality and quantity, for he is a finite creature. Human perfection, however vast and profound, has its limits, and thus there must perforce be a stage when the way of life and its regulations would cease to progress. So, contrary to the abovementioned assumption, human progress actually indicates that there must be a final and unchanging religion (as any finite motion has a terminus).

Second, to consider the Greek and Roman civilizations (which were in fact products of a pluralistic and idolatrous worldview) as Divine and super-human is to neglect the Qur'an's explicit condemnation of heathen civilizations as deviations that entail damnation. The Qur'an asserts that their ways, though they might appear virtuous, were profane, and obviously profane methods do not lead to felicity (Qur'anic verses in this regard are so numerous that there is no need to cite any particular ones here).

Third, the inauguration of a new religion in the 7th century C.E. through the ministry of the Noble Prophet itself testifies against the claim that the post-Islam human being is not in need of Divine Dispensation, especially considering Qur'an's assertion that Islam subsumes the essence of all previous Divine revelations:

"Noah and which We have also revealed to you, and which We had enjoined upon Abraham, Moses and Jesus..."[13]

God, the Exalted, underscores this truth further by referring to the final religion in His Book as *submission*, explaining that this was also the religion of Abraham and that it is the only acceptable faith, which no one may reject:

"Indeed the only religion before God is Islam [Submission]..."[14]

"Should anyone follow a religion other than Islam, it shall

---

[13] Surah al-Shawra 42:13.

[14] Surah Al 'Imran 3:19.

Chapter 1: The Way of the Primordial Human Nature [Fitrah]

never be accepted from him..."[15]

"He has...not burdened you with any hardship in the religion, the faith of your father, Abraham..."[16]

"A faithful man or woman may not, when God and His Apostle have decided on a matter, have an option in their matter..."[17]

To say that all such exhortations were specifically addressed to the Prophet and as such do not concern us is to overlook such addresses as "O people!" "O you who have faith," which explicitly address humanity or the community of the faithful at large. Accepting the argument that the post-Islam human being is not in need of a revealed religion would render meaningless all the Qur'anic encouragements to the believers and threats to those who disobey God's commands.

Could one reasonably contend that the Noble Prophet's guidance to the religion he introduced was merely a recommendation and argue that by the verse,

"Muhammad...is the Apostle of God and the Seal of the Prophets..."[18]

God intended that people were henceforth relieved from the onus of obedience to Divine Dispensation and free to proceed toward human perfection in accordance with the judgments of their intellect and that

---

[15] Surah Al 'Imran 3:85.

[16] Surah al-Hajj 22:78.

[17] Surah al-Ahzab 33:36.

[18] Surah al-Ahzab 33:40.

obedience to Islam was merely an optional matter?

To make such arguments would be to concede to the notion of democracy, on which basis social regulations derive from the majority will. However, did the Prophet ever seek to secure the consent of a majority of the Muslims prior to instituting any of the Islamic rituals—such as, the canonical prayer, fast, *zakat*, *hajj*, or *jihad*?

There is no evidence in books of history and hagiographies to support such a point of view. He did request Muslims' counsel in deciding some social issues (such as the council he convoked preceding the Uhud Battle to decide on whether the Muslim army should remain in and defend the city or leave the city to fight the enemy at a remote location), but that was only in deciding on what route to take in performing a Divine duty, not in establishing the duty itself. Obviously, consultation as to how to perform a duty is not the same as consultation as to whether the duty should be performed in the first place.

Another possible interpretation of the verse,

"Muhammad...is the Apostle of Allah and the Seal of the Prophets..."[19]

is that Islam is truly a Divine religion, but since the line of prophethood came to an end with the Prophet's ministry, it would be permissible, after the Prophet's time, to modify or supersede, in accordance with the judgments of "reason," any article of faith recognized as inexpedient considering the circumstances. The substance of this interpretation is that Divine Dispensation that is Islam is, like any other social law, liable to alteration with the passing of time and the changing of circumstances.

The early caliphs were of this opinion and actually put it to practice.

---

[19] Surah al-Ahzab 33:40.

They forbade and altered a number of religious practices that had been established by the Prophet and practiced during his lifetime. It was for this reason that writing and transmitting the Prophetic sayings was strictly forbidden in the first century A.H., while writing the Qur'an was encouraged, with the pretext of securing the honor of the Qur'an.

This point of view (i.e., the changeability of the articles of Islamic law), although favored by many scholars especially within the Sunni school of thought, is in stark contrast to the Qur'an's unequivocal assertion that the sacred religion of Islam never allows such alteration. The Qur'an lays emphasis, in agreement with the dictates of the primordial human nature, on the necessity of abiding by the Truth, warning that disobedience to the Truth will lead to nothing but perversion:

> *"So what is there after the truth except error..."*[20]
>
> *In the same vein, the Qur'an avers that Truth is in essence the end to which Islam guides and as such is inviolable:*
>
> ***"Indeed it is an august Book: falsehood cannot approach it, from before it nor from behind it, a gradually sent down revelation from the All-wise, the All-laudable."***[21]

There is no possibility of alteration in a book whose contents are immune from error and nullification. Furthermore, the Qur'an explicitly reserves for God the authority to decree law, categorically shunning the possibility of anyone else sharing in His authority:

> ***"Judgment belongs only to God. He has commanded you to***

---

[20] Surah Yunus 10:32.

[21] Surah Fussilat 41:41-42.

worship none except Him..."[22]

"What ever thing you may differ about, its judgment is with God..."[23]

Obviously, when no one other than God has the authority to decree law, it would be unreasonable to presume that human beings could rely exclusively on human reason to enact laws, independent of Divine Dispensation.

It should once again be pointed out that there are regulations in Islamic law that may be altered. These regulations fall under the authority of the Islamic ruler. The Islamic ruler may enact regulations to meet the needs of various circumstances, but only within the framework of the *shari'ah*.

The relation of the Islamic ruler with the Muslim society is similar to that of a legal guardian with the miniature society that is the family. The guardian may do whatever he deems necessary to secure the interests of the family. He may issue commands to the members of the family, if they be to the family's advantage. If family rights be encroached on, the guardian may defend the rights of the family, or, if prudence demands, remain silent. Of course, all his actions and commands must conform to the Islamic law. He may not perform an action or issue a command which conicts with Islam.

The same holds true regarding the Islamic ruler. He is empowered by Islamic law to call *jihad* to defend the safety of the Muslim nation. He may sign treaties with other states to ensure peace. Should the circumstances necessitate, whether due to war or other issues during peace, he may impose taxes. All such decisions, however, must be in the framework of Islam and in response to the needs of the times. As

---

[22] Surah Yusuf 12:40.

[23] Surah al-Shawra 42:10.

soon as the needs have been satisfied, the respective regulations expire.

To conclude, Islamic law incorporates two types of regulations: mutable and immutable, the latter constituting the *shari'ah*:

> "Certainly We gave the Children of Israel the Book, judgment and prophethood and We provided them with all the good things, and We gave them an advantage over all the nations, and We gave them manifest precepts. But they did not differ except after knowledge had come to them, out of envy among themselves. Indeed your Lord will judge between them on the Day of Resurrection concerning that about which they used to differ. Then We set you on a clear course of the Law; so follow it, and do not follow the desires of those who do not know. Indeed they will not avail you in any way against God. Indeed the wrongdoers are allies of one another, but God is the Guardian of the Godwary."[24]

The mutable regulations, which the Islamic ruler enacts to secure the interests of the Muslim nation, expire when the circumstances that had necessitated them change.

---

[24] Surah al-Jathiyah 45:16-19.

Chapter 2: Some Philosophic and Scientific Problems

An Argument for the Temporality (That is, Creation in Time) of the World

Question

One of the Imams was once asked, "What proof is there for the contingency of the world?" The Imam replied, "Behold the egg; it consists of two liquids from which both male and female chicks of various types develop. This is proof of the createdness of the world."[25] The reply seems to have convinced the questioner, for he remained silent. However, how does this reply prove the contingency of the world?

---

[25] Al-Tafsir li Abi al-Futuh al-Razi, vol. 2, p. 301.

Answer

The egg's composition of two distinct liquids and the generation of male and female chicks of various types from it indicate a higher cause. One cannot consider the numerous forms and shapes of this world, which produce so many tantalizing effects, illusory as the skeptics do. They are real: realities with distinct essences and properties. The orderly and intricate system that governs the interrelation of these realities leaves no doubt that their existence is not fortuitous and without a higher cause; they are realities contingent on a higher cause.

As the differences between the existents of this world are real, they cannot be attributed to simple and homogeneous matter. To try to salvage this hypothesis by proposing that the disparate forms may have come about by a difference in composition or motion of simple matter is in vain, for then the question will be, from where did the difference in composition and motion come? Thus, we have no choice but to conclude that the inherent dissimilarity of the various forms and shapes is due to a higher cause that transcends materiality and the material world.

The egg is no exception. Its complex combination and numerous properties evince its contingency on a higher cause. This truth holds true for all the existents and phenomena of the world, for they are all shaped out of prime matter, which is in its essence in need of a form, a shape. Thus, the entire material world with its expansive system is contingent on a higher cause.

Prophet Muhammad's superiority to other Prophets

Question

Is there any other verse in addition to *Surah al-Ahzab* 33:40 that expresses the Noble Prophet's finality and superiority in comparison to the other prophets?

Answer

In addition to the verse you have mentioned:

> "...He is the Apostle of God and the Seal of the Prophets..."[26]

there are others that proclaim the universality and perpetuality of the message of Islam. The following are some examples:

> "...And this Qur'an has been revealed to me that I may warn thereby you and whomever it may reach..."[27]
> "...Indeed it is an august Book: falsehood cannot approach it, neither from before it nor from behind it..."[28]

The claim to perpetuality of a religion would be meaningless without the finality of the bringer of the religion.

Furthermore, the following verses that aver the Qur'an's superiority to other revealed books also imply the Noble Prophet's superiority, for the Noble Qur'an is the Prophet's message, and a prophet's merit is determined by his message

---

[26] Surah al-Ahzab 33:40.

[27] Surah al-An'am 6:19.

[28] Surah Fussilat 41:41-42.

"...We have sent down the Book to you as a clarification of all things..."[29]

"We have sent down to you the Book with the truth, confirming what was before it of the Book and as a guardian over it..."[30]

"He has prescribed for you the religion which He had enjoined upon Noah and which We have also revealed to you, and which We had enjoined upon Abraham, Moses, and Jesus..."[31]

The Intercession of the Fellows of Divine Unity [Ahl Al-Tawhid]

Question

In his *"Al-Tawhid"*, Majlisi, describing the qualities of the fellows of Divine Unity, narrates the following *hadith* from the Noble Prophet:

"And verily the fellows of Divine Unity intercede [on behalf of others], and their intercession is heeded."[32]

Please explain for whom do the fellows of Divine Unity intercede? Clearly, they do not intercede for the polytheists; the monotheists, as affirmers of Divine Unity, are themselves fellows of Divine Unity. So then for whom do they intercede?

---

[29] Surah al-Nahl 16:89.

[30] Surah al-Ma'idah 5:46.

[31] Surah al-Shawra 42:13.

[32] Al-Tawhid, p. 29, hadith 31.

Answer

The above *hadith* may be construed in one of two ways. First, the "fellows of Divine Unity" may refer exclusively to the highest elite of the monotheists, the Gnostics.[33] Second, the phrase may be understood to include all monotheists. In the latter case, those interceded for will be the masses of unbelievers (who constitute the majority of humankind), the "intellectually destitute," those concerning whom God, the Exalted, says

> *"There are others waiting God's edict: He shall either punish them or turn to them clemently..."*[34]

The question of slavery in Islam

Question

In my previous correspondences, I inquired regarding Islam's approval of the continuation of the practice of slavery. You had replied in summary and for a more thorough answer had referred me to volume six of your *"Al-Tafsir al-Mizan"*. But I did not find my answer there.

Let me repeat my question. In the early years of Islam, due to certain circumstances, slavery was condoned. But then, considering that the progress of human reason would one day compel him to renounce the enslavement of human beings by other human beings as inhuman and

---

[33] This reading is supported by the following verses of the Qur'an:"Those whom they invoke besides Him have no power of intercession, except those who are witness to the truth and who know." (Surah al-Zukhruf 43:86)

[34] "...None shall speak except whom the All-beneficent permits and who says what is right." (Surah al-Naba' 78:38)Surah al-Tawbah (or Bara'ah) 9:106.

irrational, why was it allowed to endure?

If the reason for sanctioning the subjugation of infidels in captivity was to reform their souls in the Muslim community, then why were their children, although Muslim confined to bondage? To reply that Islam had at the same time established a variety of measures to facilitate their freedom would not justify its sanctioning of slavery in the first place and its subjecting many of the slave's religious matters to his master's discretion.

Answer

You write that you did not find your answer in volume six of *"Al-Tafsir al-Mizan"*; that the progressive human mind condemns slavery, which is to rob a human being of freedom; that slavery is not rational; that if Islam sanctioned the subjugation of the infidels to reform their souls in the Muslim society, for what sin were their children sentenced to the same plight in spite of their embracing Islam? To reply that Islam had established certain measures to facilitate their freedom is insufficient, for the main problem lies in sanctioning slavery in the first place. Evidently, the discussion I referred to in *"Al-Tafsir al-Mizan"* was not read with due attention. Thus, it seems necessary that I repeat the explanation.

To begin with, the human being, although endowed with the faculty of volition and thus a free creature, can never pursue his liberty uninhibited. As a social creature he is at all times bound by laws that are enacted to ensure the society's wellbeing and as such he cannot enjoy unrestrained freedom. Therefore, human liberty is always confined within the framework of laws and regulations.

In other words, human freedom is partial not absolute. Common people in a society are not free in abiding by the laws of that society. In addition to this universal restriction on freedom, there are certain circumstances that to a large extent curtail personal freedom. The insane, the mentally incompetent [*safih*], and children may not exercise even the partial freedom that sane and competent adults enjoy. In the same vein, a society's enemies and criminals are perforce deprived of their liberty.

The next issue to deal with is what bondage denotes, regardless of what word we may employ in designating it. Bondage denotes depriving an individual of freedom in making decisions and carrying them out. Obviously, the will and action of one so bound are considered the possession of another. This is the meaning of the slave trade that was so prevalent in previous times.

In pre-Islamic times, an individual could be enthralled in one of four ways: 1) the guardian of a family was entitled to sell his children into bondage, 2) a man could give his wife to another man either as a lease or as a gift, 3) the ruler of a people considered it his right to enslave at will whomever he desired (it was for this reason that kings were often referred to as "possessors of slaves"), 4) in times of war, soldiers of the vanquished army were at the mercy of the victorious party, who could enslave the enemy combatants, free them, or slay them.

Of the four ways, Islam abolished the first three by delimiting the rights of the parents and the husband and by advocating the spread of a just Islamic government. The fourth way, however, it sanctioned, for it would have been against human nature to do otherwise. No individual in his right mind would remain silent in facing an enemy intent upon effacing his identity and desecrating what he holds sacred.

Similarly, he would not, after gaining victory, let his enemy free. He would, rather, subject his enemy to captivity (another name for bondage) unless exceptional circumstances or factors call for pardon.

This has been the dictate of human nature from time immemorial and will remain so as long as human nature remains unchanged. Thus, your claim that it is against reason for one human being to subjugate another is only correct in the case of the first three ways of enslavement, as was just explicated.

You have also said that the modern human mind deplores slavery. This statement, although you may have not consciously intended so, implies that the modern world—i.e., the West—condemns undermining individual liberty, which might be supported by the fact that 80 years ago[35] and only after many a struggle a universal abolition of slavery was proclaimed, thus ostensibly removing this stigma from the face of humankind.

In doing so, the modern world held all other nations—including the Muslim nations, whose religion, it perceived, condoned slavery—beholden to it. One must, however, consider more carefully the extent to which the "humane" governments of the modern world have actually respected this universal abolition of slavery in practice.

It is true that the first two forms of slavery (i.e., selling one's children or wife), which were prevalent in Africa and some other parts of the world, have been effectively abolished (of course, 12 centuries after Islam declared them illegitimate), but have the modern governments in question put an end to the third form, which Islam abolished along with the first two? Are not the millions of Asian and African people who have been suffering under Western imperialism for centuries, robbed of their independence and the fruits of their toil, in effect slaves of the modern governments? The only difference is the reluctance to employ the word 'slavery'. But in point of fact, the harm pre modern slaveholders inicted on individuals, the modern governments inict on entire nations.

After the end of World War II, Western imperialist powers slowly granted liberty and independence to a number of their colonies whom they patronizingly deemed politically matured. But that only proved

---

[35] That is, counting back from the date 'Allamah wrote this article. [trans.]

that they claimed liberty their prerogative (to say nothing of the reality of this ostensible liberty, which was merely a new name for the same bondage disguised in a different shape, as the brand of servitude with which these modern states had smeared the face of the oppressed would not easily be erased, not even if the water of the seven seas were consumed), depriving of independence the so-called barbarous and backward nations, treating them as slaves who must, as long as they exist, serve their masters, the standard-bearers of modern civilization.

Moreover, what path have these modern states pursued vis-à-vis the fourth form of slavery—to divest of freedom prisoners of war? This question may be answered by looking at the situation that followed the Second World War. The Allied Forces, after subduing their enemies and forcing them into an unconditional surrender, poured into the enemies' countries, appropriating whatever they deemed useful of the enemies' heavy industry.

They captured of the enemy all those whom they thought useful and killed at will those they thought dangerous, enforcing their domination on the defeated nations in every respect they perceived necessary.

Today, 20 years since the end of the war, there is no indication that the subdued nations would enjoy total freedom in the near future. The problem of East Germany still persists, and German scientists are still being held in the Soviet Union against their will.

The Allied Forces did not limit their retributive measures to the adult and the able-bodied; they subjected the enemies' children, including those born after the war, to the same bondage their parents were made to suffer. The fact that the adults fought the war did not relieve the children's plight.

Their purported logic in such treatment was defending their very existence and safeguarding their future. The enemy cannot be forgiven right when it lays down its arms and yields to unconditional surrender, and its children cannot be exonerated, for subsequent generations are inextricably tied to their predecessors unless extraordinary circumstances sever such ties. This logic has been with human societies since time immemorial. It is the logic that still persists and will definitely endure, for it is unreasonable to pardon, out of pity, an enemy intent on one's destruction.

In this light, Islam has also endorsed this natural human treatment vis-à-vis prisoner of war, resolving with courtesy, honesty, and kindness what secular governments achieve ruthlessly and unscrupulously through political stratagems. Thus, Islam is correct in sanctioning the captivity of hostile infidels, in its refusal to absolve them on the basis of their alleged conversion to Islam, and in its subjecting the children to the status of their parents, while at the same time providing for their comfort and facilitating their freedom with all possible means.

Humankind's Origination from Adam and Eve

Question

Among the most troubling questions for educated believers is that of human creation. The Noble Qur'an expressly names Adam as the progenitor of the human race, emphasizing his creation from clay, whereas anthropologists, after years of research, have offered a variety of explanations regarding this question, none of which are compatible with the Qur'anic theory. The scientists' views are based on many years of research on human and animal species. We hope you may enlighten us regarding this question.

Answer

Adam and his wife being the progenitors of the existing human race is an issue stated in the Qur'an in unequivocal terms and as such cannot be construed in any figurative way unless there be definitive proof to the contrary.[36] The scientific views provided in regard to the question of the origin of the human race (such as human evolution from fish or monkeys) are merely theories that are meant for scientific purposes.

The most such theories can establish is that the existing human being is more perfect than his hypothetical origin, but this is alien to the question of the one's evolution from the other, which is what the evolutionary theorists claim.[37] But let me also add that the scientific theory that the human species has been around for millions of years is in no way at odds with the principal tenets of Islam.

Moreover, the fact that certain fossils belonging to millions of years back resemble the skeleton of the existing human being is no proof that they both belong to the same race. It is possible that Earth has passed through many cycles, each cycle having a distinct human race that became extinct at the end of that specific duration, being replaced after some time with another race of humanity. This hypothesis is corroborated by some *hadith*s that indicate that the existing human race constitutes the eighth human cycle on Earth.

---

[36] We have treated this question in "Al-Tafsir al-Mizan", in discussing the first verses of Surah al-Nisa'.

[37] In other words, the fact that sample B seems more perfect than sample A does not prove that the more perfect has evolved out of the less perfect. It only shows that B is more perfect and nothing more. [trans.]

The Difference between the Science of Psychology and Spiritual Self-Knowledge

The Difference between the Science of Psychology ['Ilm Al-Nafs] and Spiritual Self-Knowledge

[Ma'Rifah Al-Nafs]
Question

Please explain the difference between psychology [*'ilm al-nafs*] and spiritual self-knowledge [*ma'rifat al- nafs*].

Answer

Psychology is commonly used in reference to the specific science that deals with the mind, its properties, and its related issues, whereas self-knowledge refers to actually comprehending the reality of the soul through immediate spiritual vision. Psychology is rooted in *mental perception*, self-knowledge in *spiritual witnessing*.

The Definition of Self-Knowledge

Question

Is self-knowledge the spiritual witnessing of the soul divested of matter and form or does it denote something else? In any case, please clarify the meaning of "self-knowledge," which Qur'anic verses and *hadiths* so often exhort the believers to achieve.

Answer

Self-knowledge refers to the spiritual witnessing of the soul divested of matter, not of matter and form, for the spirit *is* the form. But ultimately, the purpose of self-knowledge, as mentioned in many *hadith*s, is to attain knowledge of the Lord.

The Relation between Self-Knowledge and Knowledge of God

Question

Sayyid 'Abd Allah Shubbar, in his *"Masabih al-Anwar"*, enumerates twelve different interpretations of the well-known *hadith*, "Whosoever acquires self-knowledge will indeed know his Lord."[38] Can you please shed light on this topic by explaining the relation between self-knowledge and knowledge of God?

Answer

Of the twelve interpretations you alluded to, none, if I remember correctly, approach the true meaning of the *hadith*. Only the one that employs the concept of *existential indigence* may be said to shed light on the *exoteric* meaning of the *hadith*. From the point of view of existential indigence, since the soul is an existent whose existential cause is the Exalted Truth, before Him it can have no claim to any degree of independence, for whatever it possesses belongs to Him. Therefore, one cannot look into one's soul, which so strongly reects the image of God and not see Him at the same time.

---

[38] Misbah al-Shari'ah, no. 13.

The True Meaning of Knowing and Meeting God

Question

There are numerous *hadith*s in *"Usul al-Kafi"* and *"Basa'ir al-Darajat"* regarding the creation of the Pure Imams and their luminous station. Some of these state that they were the first creatures God created.

Moreover, from a number of other *hadith*s, including *"Al-Ziyarah al-Jami'ah"*, one may infer that the Imams are the "Names of God" [*asma' Allah*], the "Face of God" [*wajh Allah*], he "Hand of God" [*yad Allah*], and the "Beside God" [*janb Allah*].

Considering such *hadith*s (especially in light of the Master of the Faithful's assertion, "To gain luminous knowledge of me is to gain knowledge of God"), can it be concluded that the true meaning of knowing God and meeting Him (topics that recur in the Qur'an and the *hadith*s) is actually acquiring knowledge of the Infallibles? Please expound how these *hadith*s may be reconciled with those that explicitly point to direct knowledge of God?

Answer

The Luminous Station of the Imams is their station of perfection, which is the highest possible state of human perfection. Their being the "Names of God", the "Face of God", the "Hand of God", and the "Beside God" is one of the profound mysteries of Divine Unity whose thorough exposition is beyond the scope of this letter.

What can be said in summary (and only by recourse to philosophical terminology) is that the Imams are the perfect manifestations of the Divine Names and Attributes. They are invested with Universal Authority [*wilayah al-kulliyyah*] and are the conduits of Divine effusion [*fayd*]. As such, to know them would be to know God, inviolable is His

Name.

Self-Knowledge: The Key to Knowledge of God

Question

In his *"Risalah Liqa'iyyah"* (A Treatise on Meeting God), Mirza Jawad Aqa Maliki Tabrizi elucidates that contemplation on self-knowledge is the key to gaining knowledge of the Lord. Taking into account the fact that the soul is an immaterial being, the question arises, can mental contemplation fathom immaterial beings? If possible, please explain in clearer terms what the honorable author of the alluded book intends.

Answer

Thought can penetrate the realm of immateriality just as it encompasses the realm of materiality. You may refer to books of philosophy, the chapter on immaterial existents, to obtain a fuller understanding of questions related to the immaterial realm. However, the meaning of *thought* in this context (i.e., spiritual perfection through introspection and self-knowledge) differs from the common acceptation. What is intended here is to retire to a quiet and secluded spot, close one's eyes, and focus on one's form as though looking into a mirror, dispelling any other thought that may spoil the mind, solely focusing on one's form.

Clarifying Two Points

Question

There are two points in *"Risalah Liqa'iyyah"* that I find troubling. The first is on the subject of contemplation to achieve self-knowledge, where the honorable author writes, "The contemplator at times engages in examining his self and at other times the world until it finally dawns upon him that the world he knows is nothing but himself and that the world is not an external one; rather, the worlds he is acquainted with are all united with himself."[39] What is the meaning of this passage? The second question relates to the passage that follows the abovementioned: "He [i.e., the contemplator] must then dispel any other thought from his heart and meditate on nothingness." What do dispelling all thoughts and reecting on nothingness actually mean?

Answer

The first passage you quoted points to the fact, which is substantiated by rational proof and which one must constantly remind oneself of, that what one comprehends of oneself and the world around him, he comprehends within himself. He does not grasp the external world as such. And to dispel all imaginary thoughts is to dismiss them in the attempt to exclusively focus by the eye of one's heart on one's form, and to contemplate nothingness is to remember the unreality, and, in essence, the nothingness of oneself.

Attaining to the Station of Self-Knowledge

---

[39] Risalah Liqa'iyyah, p. 188.

Question

Is it possible for non-Shi'ahs and, more generally, non-Muslims to attain to the spiritual station of self-knowledge through acts of worship and spiritual practices ordained by their respective religions? If possible, then obviously it would follow that they are also capable of acquiring true knowledge of God, thereby reaching the final end of the sacred religion of Islam, namely *tawhid*. This in turn would mean that one may attain to the final goal of spiritual perfection without having to traverse the path of Islam. Is this a valid assumption?

Answer

Although some scholars hold it possible, it goes against the literal reading of the Qur'an and the Sunnah[40], unless one assumes the spiritual seeker in question as "intellectually destitute" in regard to the preliminary stages of the spiritual journey.[41]

The Meaning of "Remembering God"

Question

What is intended by "remembering God," which the Qur'an so frequently exhorts the believers to maintain? Is it keeping the friends [*awliya'*] of God and His blessings in mind? Please clarify this question.

---

[40] Sunnah, with a capitol S, is used here to refer to the second source of Islamic doctrine alongside the Qur'an, which consists of the Prophet's, and, in the case of Shi'ah Islam, the Imams' sayings and conduct as recorded in books of Islamic tradition. [trans.]

[41] "Intellectually destitute" or mustad'af designates those unbelievers who are free of blame for their unfaith as they never had the chance to become aware of the truth. Such persons are commonly believed to be pardoned by God. [trans.]

Answer

The meaning of remembrance [*dhikr*] is clear, and to remember God is, at its lowest stage, to have Him in mind in what we decide to do and decide not to do, thus conforming our behavior to His will. In its higher meaning, it is to view oneself at all times before God and, higher still, to see God before oneself, of course in a manner appropriate to His Sacred Essence.

"One Cannot Bestow on others what one Lacks."

Question

If the philosophic principle that an object lacking a quality cannot bestow on others what it lacks be universally and invariably true, then how does God bestow materiality on objects while He lacks it?

Answer

The principle that one cannot bestow on others what one lacks is a philosophic one, which allows of no exception. According to this principle, every cause must encompass all the existential qualities of its effect. However, as is elaborated in books of philosophy in the chapter on *ja'l* (causation), it is solely its existence that the effect receives from its cause, not its essence.

Thus the qualities that the cause bestows on the effect are existential ones. The effect's essence, however, the cause does not possess nor is it anything related to the cause's existentiation. In this light, what God—inviolable is His Name—bestows on material existents is their positive existential qualities. Materiality is an aspect of their essence, and God is neither limited by any particular essence nor does He forge essence.⁴²

The World in Flux

Question

Is the world, from the Islamic perspective, in a state of ux?

Answer

Change and evolution in the elements of this world is obvious and indubitable. The Qur'an thus expresses this truth:

> *"We did not create the heavens and the earth and whatever is between them except with the truth and for a specified term..."*⁴³

There are numerous verses to the same effect, underscoring the truth that every phenomenon in this world possesses a distinct set of qualities and pursues a particular end, which is its perfection, and that it has a fixed point of termination, the actualization of which triggers its dissolution and disintegration into its component elements.

---

⁴² To elaborate on this topic, no doubt a complicated philosophical one, would not be possible here. You may refer to books on Islamic philosophy to pursue this discussion further. One book in particular that may be of help is "The Elements of Islamic Metaphysics", a translation by Sayyid 'Ali Quli Qara'i of the author's concise book on Islamic philosophy. [trans.]

⁴³ Surah al-Ahqaf 46:3.

Immutable Laws

Question

Does change and evolution in this world follow certain immutable principles? Or are the principles themselves also subject to change?

Answer

From the Qur'anic point of view, the order that rules the cosmos and the laws that the elements of creation follow spring from the immutable and universal Divine Norm:

> "...You will never find any change in God's Norm, and you will never find any revision in God's Norm."[44]
> "Indeed my Lord is on a straight path."[45]

The Cosmic Journey toward Perfection

Question

Has the cosmos always proceeded on a path toward perfection? According to the science of physics, the first atom, a hydrogen atom, was born around 10 billion years ago. Before that point, the world was a maelstrom of gas-like material. The elements of the cosmos grew progressively more complex and dense until galaxies were formed, one of which included the solar system, which Earth inhabited. Earth has itself undergone four stages: solidification, emergence of life, evolution

---

[44] Surah Fatir 35:43.
[45] Surah Hud 11:56.

of life-forms, and the advent of the human being.

Answer

The verses cited in answer to the previous question also hold the answer to this question. The world has had and will have, as long as it exists, a special trajectory and a certain order, directing it on its path of perfection toward its determined end.

However, the assumed figure of cosmic life cannot be accurate, for the phenomenon of time is a continuous quantity that is a concomitant of motion. Thus, every motion has its own distinct time. The conventional time we, the occupants of Earth, are familiar with, is measured by the length of day and night, for it is a unit noticeable by all people, and as such we measure according to this unit our particular events.

Priority and posteriority are categories relevant, only, when the parts of one extension of time are measured in relation to each other and as such are not applicable to events beyond that particular extension of time. Therefore, to measure the life of the world in relation to the cyclic motion of Earth is inaccurate.

Stages of Cosmic Perfection and the New Laws They Require

Question

Does each new stage of cosmic evolution institute new laws that did not exist previously (such as laws pertaining to chemical substances that came into existence after the appearance of compound matter or laws pertaining to life-forms that came into existence after the appearance of life)?

Answer

Of course, with every new development new laws emerge that previously had no application. This, however, does not violate the governing Divine Norm, as God Himself asserts in His Book:

> *"For any sign that We abrogate or remove from memories, We bring another which is better than it, or similar to it..."*[46]

And regarding the expansion of the world He says,

> *"We have built the sky with might, and indeed it is We who are its expanders."*[47]

---

[46] Surah al-Baqarah 2:106.

[47] Surah al-Dhariyat 51:47.

The Agent of Perfection in the World

Question

Is conict the agent responsible for development in the world, encompassing the tiny atom and the complex human life alike?

Answer

What can be deduced from Qur'anic verses that describe the creation of things is that the agent of development, which permeates all things from the tiny atom to the complex human being, is the natural and inherent progressive motion of each creature. Regarding human creation, for instance, the Qur'an explains:

> "[God...] perfected everything that He created, and commenced man's creation from clay. Then He made his progeny from an extract of a base uid. Then He proportioned him and breathed into him of His Spirit, and made for you the hearing, the sight, and the hearts..."[48]

There are numerous verses in the Qur'an that touch on the topic of development in relation to human beings and other creatures. And in a number of verses the ultimate end of this trajectory is identified as meeting God, the Exalted:

> "O man! You are laboring toward you Lord laboriously, and you will encounter Him."[49]

---

[48] Surah al-Sajdah 32:7-9.

[49] Surah al-Inshiqaq 84:6.

> "To God belongs the kingdom of the heavens and the earth, and toward God is the destination."[50]

The Qur'an further asserts that the origin of existence is God, and it is to Him that all creatures return in perfection:

> "God originates the creation, then He will bring it back, then you will be brought back to Him."[51]

Human Societies and the Rhythm of Perfection

Question

What are the main factors responsible for the progress of human societies?

Answer

From the Islamic viewpoint, the human being is an immortal creature, not extinguished by death. His eternal felicity, which is his existential perfection, rests on faith and righteous conduct. These two constitute his true growth and spiritual advancement:

> "Indeed man is at a loss, except those who have faith and do righteous deeds..."[52]

In other words, it is the acknowledgment of the true beliefs (which

---

[50] Surah al-Nur 24:42.

[51] Surah al-Rum 30:11.

[52] Surah al-'Asr 103:2-3.

elevates one nearer to God) and the performance of righteous deeds (which fortifies one's beliefs) that are the main factors of human progress:

"...To Him ascends the good word, and righteous conduct elevates it..."[53]

Human Progress in Science and Other Fields

Question

Is human progress limited to scientific advancement or does it include other fields as well?

Answer

From the Islamic viewpoint, the perfection of the perfect human being is in his very existence. It affects every related field and all his existential properties, and it is accompanied by knowledge. Qur'anic verses articulate the highest state of human perfection at length; one such verse is the following:

"There they will have whatever they wish, and with Us there is yet more."[54]

The verses we have cited in these discussions should suffice to prove the point (although my ill health prevented me from expanding on the meaning of the cited verses). For a better understanding of the connection of the cited verses you may refer to *"Al-Tafsir al-Mizan"*.

---

[53] Surah Fatir 35:10.

[54] Surah Qaf 50:35.

The Arguments for the Existence of Immaterial Beings

Question

What rational proof, other than *imkan-i ashraf* (the doctrine of the possibility of the more noble[55]), is there for the existence of immaterial beings?

Answer

One may consult Avicenna's books, for he did not espouse this doctrine. Moreover, there are other possible ways for proving the existence of immaterial beings (here, immaterial being denotes an existent whose action as well as essence is immaterial).

For instance, one may argue that the first existent issued from the Infinite Truth must be immaterial as it is fully actualized in its perfection, for to have any potential perfection—thus being material and comprising matter and form—would mean that its parts would be ontically prior to the whole, and as such its matter and form would be issued prior to the whole, but this is at odds with the initial assumption

---

[55] This metaphysical doctrine is cited in proof of immaterial beings that intermediate between the Infinite Truth, which is God, and the world of material existents. It contends—after assuming that material beings cannot be directly issued from God—that the existence of material existents indicates that by necessity there must be nobler existents as the direct efficient causes of the material beings. These nobler existents by virtue of their existential superiority must be immateria [trans.]

that the existent be the first issued from the Infinite Truth.⁵⁶

Another way would be to employ the immateriality of the mind's cognitive perceptions, which has been philosophically demonstrated, to prove the immateriality of the soul and in turn the soul's efficient cause.

A Rational Proof for the Termination of Prophethood

Question

Is there any rational proof for the termination of prophethood [khatm al-nubuwwah]?

Answer

In logic, in the chapter on rational demonstration [*burhan*], it is demonstrated that rational reasoning cannot render particular conclusions. Thus, particular prophethood⁵⁷ cannot be deduced by any rational reasoning, whereas general prophethood⁵⁸ may be. Nonetheless, one may reason that since the purpose of prophethood is to perfect and

---

⁵⁶ It must be noted that an immaterial being is that which is not composed of matter and form and which is fully actualized. That is, it is at its highest state of perfection from the very beginning, and as such it is immutable and not subject to evolvement. [trans.]

⁵⁷ That is, the Divine ministry of a particular prophet. It is, however, largely used in reference to that of Prophet Muhammad. [trans.]

⁵⁸ That is, prophethood in general: the doctrine that God appoints certain human beings to act as messengers between Him and humankind, without reference to any particular prophet. [trans.]

Chapter 2: Some Philosophic and Scientific Problems

guide human beings, it takes on different forms (hence, the plurality of Divine Dispensations) corresponding to the progressive development of humankind, each successive form presenting a more perfect degree that supercedes its predecessor.

However, as the human being is obviously not infinite in his capacity to achieve perfection, no matter how numerous the perfections he is capable of attaining, there is a point where he will cease to go further. Naturally, the particular Divine Dispensation that encompasses this climax of human perfection would be the termination of prophethood and as such would endure as the binding law of God until the Day of Judgment.

> *The Noble Qur'an, the heavenly book of the sacred religion of Islam, explicitly testifies that Prophet Muhammad is the Seal of the Prophets and that the Qur'an is the final indissoluble book of God:*
>
> **"... [Muhammad] is the apostle of God and the Seal of the Prophets..."**[59]
>
> **"...Indeed [the Qur'an] is an august book: falsehood cannot approach it, neither from before it not from behind it, a gradually sent down revelation from One All-wise, All-laudable."**[60]

Hence, Prophet Muhammad being the Seal of the Prophets and the Qur'an the Seal of all Divine Dispensations is thus demonstrated.

An additional point that the above explanation clarifies is that the termination of prophethood in no way implies that the human being has reached a point of intellectual sufficiency where he is no

---

[59] Surah al-Ahzab 33:40.

[60] Surah Fussilat 41:41-42.

longer in need of Divine Dispensation, for in such a case the manifold instructions of Islam would be in vain.

Distinguishing 'Idalah from 'Ismah

Distinguishing *'idalah* (Uprightness)[61] from *'ismah* (Infallibility)

Question

What is the distinction between *"idalah"* and *"ismah"* in prophets who, unlike angels, are susceptible to anger and lust?

Answer

'Idalah is the state of mind that empowers one to refrain from committing the major sins and repeating the minor sins but is not strong enough to prevent the isolated commission of minor sins. *'Ismah*, on the other hand, is the state of mind that renders one immune from committing any sin whatsoever, whether major or minor.

This state of mind, according to Qur'anic verses, is of the nature of knowledge—the knowledge of the awfulness of sin—the possession of which makes the commission of sin impossible. It may be likened to one's knowledge that a liquid is lethally poisonous, which would definitely prevent one from drinking that liquid. Thus, with *'idalah* one may sin but not with *'ismah*.

---

[61] *'Idalah* is a technical term in Islamic law that indicates the degree of piety that prevents one from committing the major sins and repeating the minor sins. [trans.]

The Impossibility of Violating Ontic Reality [Takwin]

Question

The grounds for the doctrine of the absolute infallibility of prophets, one of the unquestionable tenets of the Shi'ah faith, cannot include such mundane matters as a simple chitchat with one's wife, for instance. But assuming that the prophets are inerrant even in such matters, the state of *'idalah* would be sufficient to explain it.

Thus, even if there is sufficient evidence for this doctrine, it would only serve to prove infallibility solely in the scope of the duties that pertain to the Divine ministry—i.e., being immune from error and negligence in passing the Divine Dispensation to the people—but not in regard to other sins. Furthermore, what is the reason for this insistence on proving this doctrine? Would the prophethood of an *'adil*[62]—but not infallible—prophet entail any adverse consequences?

Answer

Based on the rational argument that proves the necessity of general prophethood, the guidance of humankind is part of the order of creation, of reality. As there is no possibility of error and contravention in reality, the contents of Revelation, emanating from the wellspring of Divine Knowledge, reach humankind intact. Hence, the prophet, as the conduit of Revelation, is immune from error and perfidy in receiving the Revelation, preserving it, and conveying it to the people. This requires that he be infallible in his speech and conduct, as conduct is also a means of guidance.

---

[62] 'Adil, subjective form, refers to one who possesses the quality of 'idalah. [trans.]

It can, therefore, be concluded that the prophet is untouched by sin, whether minor or major, in speech and conduct, prior to and following his ministry, for each of these states affects the conveyance of the articles of faith, and as sin is meaningless beyond these states, the prophet's infallibility is proven. This topic, however, has other dimensions for which you may refer to the third volume of *"Al-Tafsir al-Mizan"*, *"Shi'ah dar Islam"* [The Shi'ah in Islam][63], or *"Risalah Wahy wa Shu'ur-i Marmuz"* [A Treatise on Revelation, the Mysterious Intelligence].

The Meaning of the Prayer "[O God] Elevate His Status" Uttered In Tashahhud

Question

Islamic philosophers state that the perfect human being is he who has actualized "all that is generally possible for him." And all Muslims unanimously agree that Muhammad was either the only perfect man or in the ranks of the perfect men. Considering this truth, what could be the purpose of uttering the prayer "[O God] elevate [Muhammad's] status" in *tashahhud*?

Answer

The above prayer and similarly *salawat*[64] are prayers to God whose acceptance by Him is certain. They are actually expressions of one's satisfaction at God's special favor to His messenger and beloved, Muhammad.

---

[63] Translated into English by Sayyid Husayn Nasr. [trans.]

[64] The ritual utterance of blessing on Muhammad and his progeny. [trans.]

Chapter 2: Some Philosophic and Scientific Problems

Additional Answers to Previous Questions

May God's peace and blessings be upon you. Your second letter was received. I must express my most sincere gratitude for your blessings. In regard to the answers to your questions, you say that they are incomplete. Apparently, you did not consider the answers duly.

You write, "We desire the proof for immaterial beings for the guidance of corrupted youths who deny the existence of God and any supernatural being, whereas the provided answer presupposes God's existence."

The Question in hand is a philosophical one that has been demonstrated in many ways. The answer that I gave in the letter was based on the immateriality of our mental perceptions, which lack the general properties of matter—i.e., changeability and subjection to time and space. The second premise it to demonstrate the immateriality of the human soul by pointing out that one descries one's self as an unchanging entity and that the immaterial mental perceptions come into existence through the soul.

Once this is proven, we may then continue to prove the immateriality of the efficient cause of the human soul by arguing that a cause must of necessity be existentially superior to its effect; material existence is existentially inferior to immaterial existence. This argument is a sound rational demonstration, in no way contingent on the presupposition of God's existence. However, as you intend the answer for persons without advance education in philosophy, it must be rendered in an easier fashion, more acceptable to the general public.

You write, "The rational argument you have offered in the letter for the termination of prophethood is sufficiently cogent, but the cited Qur'anic verses are incapable of proving the point, for if there were to be a final religion after Islam, it would be a truth that would approach the present religion, whereas the verse in question (41:41-42) indicates that 'falsehood cannot approach it' [which leaves open the possibility of truth—that is, another Divine religion—approaching it, hence Islam not being the final Divine Dispensation]." The answer is, "falsehood" in the verse in question refers to any false statement, incompatible with the final religion of Islam, that may find its way into the Qur'an, and as such the verse does not imply, in any way, the possibility of another true Divine religion.

You write, "*Tashri'*[65] requires nothing more than conveying God's message without contravention or error, which may be accomplished by simply an *'adil* messenger. Thus infallibility is not a necessary quality for a prophet. What is enweaved in the reality of the cosmic reality [*takwin*] is the Divine Dispensation and its conveyance, not the details of life. As such trivialities of life as the Prophet's chitchat with his wife do not fall within the scope of Divine Dispensation; the Prophets' infallibility in relation to such trivialities cannot be demonstrated by recourse to the cosmic reality [*takwin*]."

What is meant by "reality" is the realm of origination [*ijad*] and ontic existence. To acknowledge that the human being's existence is willed by God, one must also accept that his existential properties—including his cosmic purpose and the way he must traverse to attain to that purpose (which must be indicated by God Himself, hence Revelation and prophethood)—are all incorporated by the cosmic reality [*takwin*].

Thus, it would be unreasonable to claim that Divine Dispensation alone is part of the cosmic reality, excluding the details of human exis-

---

[65] In Islamic theology, tashri' refers to God's revelation of Divine Dispensation to humankind for the purpose of guiding them to the Truth. As mentioned above, God's will in guiding humankind (also referred to as the doctrine of general prophethood) is part of the cosmic reality. That is, God has embedded in the cosmic order certain signposts in order to direct humanity to the True Destination, Himself. This is what 'Allamah intends when he says that "general prophethood" or tashri' is "enweaved in the reality of the universe." [trans.]

tence and the practical need for preaching the Divine Dispensation[66] from the matrix of cosmic reality and relegating them to the position of conventional and contractual issues[67].

To thus dissociate Divine Dispensation from the practical need to convey it is analogous to arguing that the human need for food is a reality while the particular instances of food consumption (e.g., "I need to eat rice" "Let me have some soup") are illusions of the human mind. It is similarly unreasonable to contend that, although a prophet's speech and conduct are factors that contribute to guidance, yet the quality of 'idalah is sufficient to render a prophet an exemplar for the guidance of humankind. For, 'idalah leaves open the possibility of committing minor or even major sins.

You further state, "It would not be injurious to the guidance of humankind if a prophet, in the secrecy of his home, backbites about others in chatting with his wife." This is most astonishing. Is not the prophet's wife one of the people whom should be guided? Or, would you differentiate between a major sin when committed secretly in the presence of one or two of one's confidants and when committed publicly?

In a word, to consider the quality of 'idalah, in lieu of infallibility, sufficient for a prophet would be to accept the possibility that a prophet may commit minor or even major sins in his speech or conduct, which is to say that he is vulnerable to violating the sanctity of his ministry in every matter of faith. This is at odds with the truth that the position

---

[66] "The details of human existence and the practical need for preaching the Divine Dispensation": in this sentence 'Allamah' is referring to the necessity of infallibility to guard every speech and action of the Prophet, as they are indispensable factors in the process of conveying the Divine message and guiding humankind to the true religion of God. [trans.]

[67] That is, things that pertain to human transactions, which would mean that they are outside the responsibility of the Prophet's ministry. [trans.]

of prophethood springs from the very reality of the cosmic order.

You write, "The prayer '[O God] elevate [the Prophet's] status' uttered during *tashahhud* unequivocally indicates the Prophet's deficiency, which the prayer is intended to ameliorate. [Thus, the explanation furnished above to the effect that such prayers are only an expression of our heartfelt happiness for the Prophet's spiritual perfection is unfounded.]" But I again reiterate that God has bestowed on the Noble Prophet the highest perfection possible for a contingent being [i.e., any being other than God].

Nevertheless, this bestowal in no way limits His omnipotence, for He is capable of taking away, at will, what He has bestowed:

> *"...Say, 'Who can avail anything against God should He wish to destroy the Messiah, son of Mary, and his mother, and everyone upon the earth...'"*[68]

Hence, one may say that the prayer in question is to ask for the continuation of this Divine effusion. Prayer, even when in relation to a determined truth, is appropriate. Thus, it is true that the prayer in question is unequivocal regarding the Prophet's imperfection; nevertheless, the imperfection at issue is the existential indigence inherent in all contingent beings.

The Purpose in Translating Greek Philosophy

Question

Greek philosophy was introduced to the Muslim World several centuries after the advent of Islam through Arabic translations. What

---

[68] Surah al-Ma'idah 5:17.

was the purpose of this translation campaign? Was it merely to acquaint Muslims with new sciences or was it a pretext for preventing Muslims from benefiting from the knowledge of the *Ahl al-Bayt*, the true guardians of Revelation?

Answer

Metaphysics was one of the many fields of knowledge—including such other sciences as logic, natural sciences, mathematics, medicine—that were introduced to Muslims from the Hellenic World through Arabic translations of Greek and Syrian works. Thus, whereas in the 1st century A.H. the caliphs of the time strictly forbade the writing of anything other than the verses of the Qur'an (including Prophetic *hadiths* and Qur'anic exposition) in the following centuries, as recorded in books of history, close to two hundred books, covering every science of the time were translated into Arabic.

This was done purportedly with the intention of strengthening the Muslim nation and actualizing the Islamic ideals, in line with the Qur'an's emphasis on intellectuality and its encouragement to study all aspects of God's creation in the heaven and on the earth, regarding other animals as well as the human being.

This is not, however, to deny that the contemporary rulers would seize every opportunity to damage the *Ahl al-Bayt*'s status within the Muslim nation so as to deprive Muslims of the Divine knowledge of the *Ahl al-Bayt*. In this light, it may be correct to say that the translation of Greek philosophy into Arabic was undertaken for the purpose of isolating the *Ahl al-Bayt*. But does this unjustifiable intention of the rulers of the time and their exploitation of the translation of Greek works of philosophy make engagement in metaphysical discussions a vanity? Is this historical reality a legitimate reason for us to refrain from dwelling on such discussions?

Philosophy includes a variety of discussions that lead to proving the existence of the Omnipotent Designer, the Necessary Existent, His Unity, as well as the other Divine Attributes. It also deals with other such related topics as the doctrines of prophethood and Resurrection. These are questions that constitute what we term the "pillars of faith," which must be rationally demonstrated in order to secure the credibility of the contents of the Qur'an and the Sunnah.

Otherwise, to seek to prove the credibility of the Qur'an and the Sunnah based on their own claims would be erroneous as it would constitute a circular argument. It is for this reason that where the Qur'an and the Sunnah deal with the principles of faith—such as God's existence and His Unity and Lordship—they furnish rational arguments.

Islamic Doctrine not in Need of Greek Philosophy

Question

Does Islam (in the broad sense, which encompasses the *"sunnah"* of the Infallibles) contain what Greek philosophy brought to the Muslim World? If it does, then what need is there for such a philosophy. If, however, it does not, then it is an imperfect religion that is in need of Greek philosophy.

Answer

Islamic sources—the contents of the Qur'an and the Sunnah—encompass all the elements necessary for the guidance of humankind, both in doctrine and in practice. Some of these elements find expression in detail and some are presented in brief. This is due to the fact that Islam addresses all people from all walks of life—the scholar and the layperson, the perceptive and the not-so-perceptive, the city-dweller and the country-dweller, man and woman. To embrace all people, Islam employs a language that is comprehensible to all so that all people could benefit from it in accordance with their varying intellectual capacities.

To benefit at a higher level from doctrines so presented, so as to arrive at truths fathomable only to the more elevated minds, one would obviously have to arrange them in a certain order and to coin terms critical to this intellectual endeavor. In this light, although the Qur'an and the Sunnah do provide metaphysical principles, there is still the need for establishing an independent science that would treat of these doctrines at a higher level.

This holds true not only in respect to philosophy but also to every other Islamic science. A good example in this regard is the science of theology, whose main elements are to be found in the Qur'an and the Sunnah; nevertheless, it has been arranged as a distinct field of knowledge.

Moreover, you claim that if the Qur'an and the Sunnah lack some metaphysical topic, it would mean that Islam is deficient and in need of Greek philosophy. This, however, is an incorrect assumption. The incorrectness of this assumption may be demonstrated by considering the case of logic. Not even a single doctrine can be deduced without the application of the rules of logic, none of which are to be found in the Qur'an and the Sunnah.

Also, in regard to the practical rules of faith, not one question may be dwelt on without recourse to the science of *usul*, although there is no trace of this vast science in the Qur'an and the Sunnah. The solution to this problem lies in the fact that the relation of logic to Islamic doctrine and that of the science of *usul* to questions of jurisprudence is one of method. To apply a particular method to a body of data is fundamentally different from adding something to it.

The Consummation of Islamic Philosophy in Mulla Sadra's Metaphysics

Question

Owing to the persistence of Shi'ah scholars in furthering the rational sciences, Islamic philosophy reached its climax in the age of Mulla Sadra. A question that comes to mind in this regard is, do the concepts that Mulla Sadra developed in *"Asfar"* and in other books have their roots in the Qur'an and the Sunnah or are they concepts external to but concordant with Islam?

Answer

In saying that Islamic philosophy reached a climax in the thought of Mulla Sadra, we mean that in comparison to prior developments of philosophy, it stands out at a much higher level and that it is more conducive to fathoming the True Knowledge. It should not, however, be inferred that Sadrian works on metaphysics—*"Asfar"*, *"Manzumah"*, and the like—reect the truth awlessly and without any error. Like any other book, they may contain errors in their contents. One should at all times seek sound rational arguments without any concern for famous names.

The Relation Between the Thought of Muslim Philosophers and Sages and Islamic Doctrine [69]

Question

If philosophy reects the teachings of the Qur'an and the *hadiths*—which no doubt surpass the former in soundness and comprehensiveness—then why seek the teachings of the philosophers and sages?

Answer

When we say that there is no difference between philosophy and the essence of the Qur'an and the Sunnah, we mean that philosophy rephrases the fundamental doctrines of the Truth—which are expressed in the Qur'an and the Sunnah in a simple and generally understandable fashion—in the format of discursive reasoning, employing the specialized vernacular of philosophers. Hence, what distinguishes the two is that one is generally comprehensible whereas the other is expressed in a specialized language.

Expounding the Hadiths That Denounce Philosophy

---

[69] Doctrine in this context consists of the verses of the Qur'an and the Tradition [sunnah] of the Infallibles.

Question

There are certain *hadith*s recorded in *"Bihar al-Anwar"* and *"Hadiqah al-Shi'ah"* that condemn philosophers, especially those of the "End of Time". To whom do such *hadith*s refer, and what do they mean?

Answer

The *hadith*s in question, which number no more than two or three (whose authenticity is questionable), denounce philosophers and not philosophy per se, just as there are similar *hadith*s that condemn Muslim jurists of the "End of Time," not the science of jurisprudence as such. There are also *hadith*s that criticize the Muslims and the readers of the Qur'an[70] who will come at the "End of Time" without, obviously, detracting in any way from the value of Islam and the Qur'an.

Moreover, to consider these *hadith*s directed at philosophy per se would in effect be an attack on the Qur'an and the Sunnah, for, as mentioned above, philosophy dwells on the same topics, the only difference being that it presents them in the form of rational reasoning and without the burden of obligation. Let me also add that it is unreasonable to dismiss definitive apodictic reasoning in favor of dubitable reports?

The Relation of Spiritual Purification with Social Involvement

---

[70] An example is, "[At the End of Time] from Islam there will remain only a name and from the Qur'an merely words." [Bihar al-Anwar 36: 284]

Question

In studying the history of Islam, one finds that the followers of Imam ʿAli were of two temperaments from the point of view of social involvement. There were those who abandoned the turbulence of social upheavals to remain in seclusion, dedicating their life solely to reforming and purifying their soul. *Uways al-Qarani* and *Kumayl* were such figures. Of these men, some were martyred at the hands of the tyrants of the time and some lived a spiritual life until God embraced them at their natural death.

On the other hand, there were those followers of ʿAli—prominent among them Malik al-Ashtar—who took up an active role in the public events of the time. This difference in attitude has also found manifestation in recent history. Men like Mulla Husayn Hamadani and his pupils pursued the first lifestyle, whereas such scholars as Muhammad Husayn Kashif al-Ghita' engaged in a more social life. The question that this comparison raises is: should spiritual purification be sought in the midst of society or in a reclusive and isolated lifestyle? Which of the two methods is preferable and more effective in advancing the cause of Islam?

Answer

What we can say with certainty based on the Qur'an and the Sunnah is that the objective of worship in Islam is to advance in the stages of Divine Knowledge and to attain sincerity in worshipping God. This journey requires that we sever all attachments except our attachment to Him—inviolable is His Name. This is the path of perfection that Islam sets forth. It is so valuable that to succeed in attaining to even the lowest stages of this journey is a praiseworthy achievement.

> "...Be wary of God with the wariness due to Him..."[71]
> "So ee toward God. Indeed I am a manifest Warner to you from Him."[72]

However, it must be pointed out that Islam is a social religion that rejects monasticism and isolation. It exhorts the believers to engage in spiritual purification, to strengthen their faith, and to enhance their knowledge of God, all in the midst of the society, while interacting with other people.

This was the approach that the devout Muslims of the early period of Islam—who had the privilege of living at the time of the Noble Imams and of receiving their guidance—embraced. Salman al-Farsi—who according to the Master of the Faithful possessed a very high degree of faith—is a good example; he was the governor of Mada'in for several years. Uways al-Qarani, the exemplar of Islamic piety, was martyred in the Battle of Siffin, fighting for the Master of the Faithful.

The Question of the Creation of the Universe

Question

Considering that God's existence—Magnificent and Exalted is He—is infinite and that it pervades all space, even prior to the creation of the finite universe, how then did the universe come about? Was the universe created within the limits of God's existence? That would be impossible. If, however, the universe was created beyond the limits of His Most Sacred Existence, it would be detached from Him; this would also be impossible. Another alternative that may be put forth—in Him

---

[71] Surah Al 'Imran 3:102.

[72] Surah al-Dhariyat 51:50.

do we seek refuge—is that His Existence is one and the same with other existents? But this entails the blasphemous theory of *monism*. So, the question is, how did God create the universe without it coming into conict with His Sacred Existence?

Answer

Well, in the first place, the question is awed. The question begins by assuming that God's infinitude is a matter of space. It must be noted; however, that prior to creation of matter, there was no space. Second, the questioner incorrectly interprets God's infinitude to mean that He is a limitless body, that He is composed of an infinitely large body that occupies all space, leaving no room for others. God's Sacred Existence, however, transcends corporeality, materiality, and material dimensions.

Thus, space and time are meaningless in relation to His existence; He does not have an inside or an outside; neither is He within anything nor is He external to anything. Such relative concepts are properties of matter, and hence God's creatures are not contained within Him, are not external to Him, and are not identical with Him. He is their Creator, and they His creatures.

Moreover, in describing God's existence as infinite, we mean that it is not contingent on any prior condition. And in saying that He is *with* His creatures, we mean that His knowledge, power, and will encompass the cosmos, not that He shares the same space with them.

The Superiority of the Station of Imamate to That of Prophethood

Question

In the story of Prophet Abraham we are taught that God conferred the status of imamate on him (who was already a prophet) only after "completing the terms" and succeeding in all the tests He set before him. How is the status of imamate superior to prophethood? And granted that it is superior, then why is there consensus among all Muslims that the Prophet was more elevated in status than 'Ali?

Answer

When God said to Abrham,

> "...I am making you the Imam of mankind..."[73]
> he was already a prophet—one of the "Ulu al-'Azm"[74]. He had brought for humankind a new book and a new Divine Law from God. This means that when God conferred on him the position of imamate, he had already been entrusted with the duty of guiding and preaching to humankind. Moreover, in His Book, God in several instances describes an "imam" as one who is responsible for the guidance of humankind.
> "...We made them Imams who guide by Our command..."[75]

Juxtaposing the above two points, it becomes clear that the guidance that an *imam* is responsible for is different from that for which a

---

[73] Surah al-Baqarah 2:124.

[74] The highest rank of prophethood. It refers to the Divine ministry of Noah, Abraham, Moses, Jesus, and Muhammad, the prophets whom were entrusted with a Divine Law. [trans.]

[75] Surah al-Anbiya' 21:73.

prophet is responsible. The guidance that is the responsibility of a prophet is to preach and to exhort people to embrace the true faith. That is, it is a prophet's duty to shed light on the true path of guidance. The duty of an *imam*, on the other hand, is to shepherd humankind toward the True Destination.

Thus, in addition to explicating the doctrines and practices of faith, an *imam* is in charge of correcting the conduct of the believers. He oversees the spiritual growth of the believers and directs their deeds in the way of God so that their actions would lead to the desirable end.

This interpretation of an *imam*'s status is supported by a number of Islamic tenets. Shi'ahs believe that the record of the conduct of all believers is submitted to the Imam of the Time on a number of occasions; that the Imam is present at the death of all people; that the Imams hand out the records of conduct to people on the Day of Judgment; and that they are the yardsticks according to which the conduct of all others is measured.

Moreover, according to Shi'ah belief, the universe would cease to exist in the absence of an *imam*. All this proves that the Prophet was also the *imam* of his time. And as the Prophet was entrusted with three simultaneous ministries—*nubuwwah*[76], *risalah*[77], and *imamah*—his rank was above that of 'Ali. This is definitively attested to by the consensus of all Muslims.

---

[76] The lowest rank of prophethood: the holder of this position is not given a new Divine Law [shari'ah] and is very limited in the scope of his ministry. [trans.]

[77] The higher rank of prophethood: it subsumes those prophets who brought a new Divine Dispensation and those who, although not entrusted with a Divine Dispensation, had more authority than a nabi—the prophet of the lowest rank who holds the status of nubuwwah. Examples of the latter class are David and Solomon. [trans.]

God, the Creator of All Creatures

Question

Some say that all creatures derive from the wellspring of God's existence, and thus the entirety of the cosmos, viewed in this unitive light, is God. But how could this be true considering the variety of creatures we observe?

Answer

The rational arguments that substantiate the existence of the Creator, describe the universe as His "action" and Him as the agent of this action. Without doubt, an action is not identical with its agent; otherwise, it would require that a thing exist prior to its coming into existence,[78] which is impossible. Hence, the universe is distinct from God, and thus to say "the entirety of the cosmos viewed in this unitive light is God" is incorrect.

Existents: Merely a Figment of the Imagination?

Question

Some are of the opinion that what we see—trees, stones, people, etc.—is only an illusion. Our existence is also just an illusion. Can you please address this problem?

---

[78] "A thing exist prior to its coming into existence": what this means is that if the agent and the action are identical, then the action already exists as the agent, and this is obviously impossible, for an effect is existentially posterior to its cause. [trans.]

Answer

To say that what we see and hear is an illusion is self-defeating, for then this proposition would itself be an illusion and thus devoid of any value. Those who make such claims are either insane or maliciously spreading corrupt thoughts through deceitful sophistry. No one, in his right mind, would doubt the reality of the world. Even those who claim this world an illusion do not abide by their claim in practice; they pursue orderly lives; when hungry and thirsty, the idea that the world is an illusion does not dissuade them from seeking water and bread.

Question

Atheists argue that assuming that this world is in fact real, what place does God hold? Does He reside in between the objects of this world? What is your reply to such skepticism?

Answer

As was explained above, such claims are at odds with rational reasoning and lack any logical ground.

The Substance of God's Existence

Question

Some say, "We have reached the conclusion that *we* [the things of this world] are the substance of God's existence, and thus to say, 'God has created us ex nihilo' is meaningless. He is nothing other than existence [which takes the shape of the existents that populate our world]. There is no other meaningful interpretation for the concept of God. The various and changing forms we see around us constitute God." What is your response?

Answer

What you have quoted is an unfounded claim, an irrational contention. Whatever they may say is good only for them and must not worry others. Such baseless claims carry no weight.

The Sufis' Remark Concerning the Qur'anic Statement "He Is the First and He Is the Last"

Question

Some Sufis are of the opinion that the pronoun in the verse,

> *"He is the First and the Last."*[79]

refers to 'Ali. A number of *hadith*s recorded by 'Allamah Majlisi in the eighth volume of *"Bihar al-Anwar"* supports this reading. This complicates the problem, for to repudiate the Sufis' interpretation would be to doubt the authenticity of the *hadith*s in question. But the truth is that there are many similar pronouns in the Qur'an whose antecedent is undoubtedly God:

> *"...It is He who guides me."*[80]

---

[79] Surah al-Hadid 57:3.

[80] Surah al-Shu'ara' 26:78.

> "...It is He who cures me."[81]
>
> "It is He who is God in the sky, and God on the earth; and He is the All-wise, the All-knowing."[82]
> "...He is the All-exalted, the All-great."[83]
>
> "...The Living One who does not die..."[84]

There are many such pronouns in the Qur'an whose context indicates that they refer to God. So how can we determine whether the antecedent in the verse the Sufis cite is 'Ali or God?

Answer

> *The* hadiths *that 'Allamah Majlisi narrates assert that 'Ali is the first and the last. What this means is clarified by another* hadith *that says that 'Ali was the first person to embrace Muhammad's faith and the last to depart him (he buried the Prophet's sacred body). But leaving these* hadiths *aside, the verse in question (57:3) seems to be indicating God, Who has always been and will always be.*
>
> **"Indeed toward your Lord is the journey."**[85]

---

[81] Surah al-Shu'ara' 26:80.
[82] Surah al-Zukhruf 43:84.
[83] Surah al-Hajj 22:62.
[84] Surah al-Furqan 25:58.
[85] Surah al-Najm 53:42.

The Necessary Existent [Wajib], the Originating Cause of All Contingent Existents [Mumkinat]

Question

Let me, with all due respect, ask you a question that occurred to me after reading the chapter entitled, "A Philosophic Discussion" that appears in volume 15 of *"Al-Tafsir al-Mizan"*, pp. 149-150. There you state that in the creation of contingent beings, God is a "partial cause."[86] But how is this conceivable in light of the Qur'an's assertion that

> *"...Nothing is like Him..."*[87]

Answer

Your question refers to the philosophic discussion presented in volume 15, pp. 149-150, of *"Al-Tafsir al- Mizan"*, where I have offered two viewpoints regarding God's agency in creating contingent beings.

According to the first viewpoint, God is a partial cause, whereas the second viewpoint acknowledges God as the complete cause. These two viewpoints are not, as might be assumed, in opposition to one

---

[86] This philosophic term refers to a cause that is necessary but not self-sufficient in actualizing a particular effect. For instance, an architect is a partial cause, for he is only one of the factors necessary for constructing a building. Many other factors are required in order to complete the construction of the building. Partial cause contrasts with complete cause, a cause that is independent in bringing about a particular effect, such as God's agency in engendering the First Creature. [trans.]

[87] Surah al-Shawra' 42:11.

another; only the second one is more accurate and better formulated.

The first viewpoint observes the phenomena of this world in their outward appearance. When viewing this world prima facie, there is an evident multiplicity and separation among phenomena. Of the phenomena of this world, some are existentially prior to others. This reality is the foundation of the universal principle of causality.

According to this principle every contingent being is in need of a cause that, if contingent, in turn needs a higher cause. This chain continues until it reaches the Essentially Necessary Existent, God, who is Self- sufficient. He is the source from which all contingent beings issue, whether directly (in the case of the First Emanation) or indirectly. From this perspective, God is a partial cause—one component of the efficient cause—vis-à-vis His indirect effects. This is the superficial viewpoint.

From the second viewpoint, all contingent beings are bound together by an ontic dependency that is the result of the principle of causality. Thus, they form an organic whole, and God is the complete cause of this whole. This line of reasoning is based on the truth that the creation of the first contingent being—the First Emanation—is equivalent to the origination of all contingent beings, as elucidated in *"Al-Tafsir al-Mizan"*.

Without doubt, the second viewpoint is grounded on a firmer foundation. Nevertheless, it should be pointed out that to consider God a partial cause does not contradict the Qur'an's assertion that *"...Nothing is like Him..."* for to ascribe causality to contingent beings as conduits for Divine effusion, which He Himself has established, does not imply that they are analogous in causality to Him. God's agency is essential and independent whereas theirs is accidental and dependent.

This also applies to other attributes of perfection[88]—e.g., powerful, living, knowing, hearing, seeing—whose attribution to contingent beings does not constitute polytheism. The attributes of perfection that exist within the realm of contingent beings are engendered and effused by the Necessary

Existent and so depend on Him. God, however, possesses the attributes of perfection as the Essentially Independent and Self-Sufficient Being.

It may be objected that the ascription of causality to God's creatures runs against the Qur'anic verse,

"...Is there any creator other than God..."[89]

This, however, is not correct. What is intended by this verse is that God is independent in His creation, creating the world without recourse to any other agent, whereas other "creators" are in need of Him.

This latter understanding is verified by the Qur'an itself where it confirms that there are other "creators" beside God. Among the verses to this effect are the following:

"So blessed is God, the best of creators."[90]
"...And when you [i.e., Jesus Christ] would create from clay the form of a bird, with My leave, and you would breathe into it and it would become a bird, with my leave..."[91]

---

[88] Attributes of perfection are contrasted with negative attributes. The former are those positive existential qualities whose ascription to God does not delimit Him in any way. [trans.]

[89] Surah Fatir 35:3.

[90] Surah al-Mu'minun 23:14.

[91] Surah al-Ma'idah 5:110.

This reading is further corroborated by the Qur'an where it alludes to the universal principle of causality

> *"..And commenced man's creation from clay. Then He made his progeny from an extract of base uid."*[92]
> *"... [God] created you from a single soul, and created its mate from it, and, from the two of them, scattered numerous men and women..."*[93]

(It should be noted that the absolute negation of causality from contingent beings and reserving it exclusively for God is a notion held by Ash'ari theologians—a notion they cannot substantiate.)

Origination of Matter Preceded by Temporal Non-Existence

Origination of Matter Preceded by Temporal Non-Existence ['Adam Zamani][94]

Question

On what grounds are matter's essential eternity [qidam dhati] negated?

---

[92] Surah al-Sajdah 32:7-8.

[93] Surah al-Nisa' 4:1.

[94] Temporal nonexistence ['adam zamani] refers to a time when something did not exist. Here the questioner is essentially asking whether there was a time when matter did not exist. [trans.]

Answer

The term *essential eternity* applies to an existent that is free of the limitations of a delimited essence. It is impossible for such an existence to experience nonexistence, and consequently it is not susceptible to change in its essence, properties, or states. Obviously, matter does not fit this description. So, apparently your question is actually regarding temporal eternity [*qidam zamani*] not essential eternity.[95] So, the question may be rephrased more accurately in this way: was there a time when matter (composed of atoms) did not exist? The answer is positive.

As demonstrated in physics, atom can be transformed into energy and vice versa.

Atom is composed of concentrated particles of energy, and as such atom is preceded by nonexistence. Based on this scientific fact, there must be a common material from which both matter and energy derive, whose sole property is receptivity to form, which gives it actuality. And since it is implausible that the form-giver (i.e., the agent that bestows form and actuality on the common material, that is, prime matter) be the prime matter in question, there must of necessity be an existent transcending matter, to which matter is indebted for its form and actualization. Thus, the sensible world of existence is the activity of an eternal, immutable, and transcendent agent, that is, God—inviolable is

---

[95] Islamic philosophers distinguish between two types of eternity: essential eternity [qidam dhati] and temporal eternity [qidam zamani]. The former is used in reference to a necessary being whose nonexistence is rationally impossible as it is self-sufficient in its existence. The latter describes a contingent being that is eternal but not by virtue of its essential self- sufficiency. [trans.]

His Name.[96]

The Existence of Evil

Question

In the world we inhabit, evil is all-pervasive; the human and the brute alike oppress the weak to the most extreme limits. We have all witnessed the awful scene of a weaker animal falling prey to the stronger predacious animal, which ends the life of the innocent prey in a most brutal fashion. Moreover, there is the question of those oppressed without an oppressor, such as children who come to this world with a congenital disability.

Answer

Before giving an answer, I would like to draw your attention to an introductory point. The order of creation has been founded on the principle of cause and effect; the cosmos is governed by existential principles—not by sentiment—that allow of no exception. For instance, the property of fire is that it burns whatever it comes in contact with, be it the dress of a prophet or the attire of a tyrant. Carnivorous animals perish if deprived of meat, thus they must prey on other animals. This is what the order of creation has embedded in their biological construction, and so they are not guilty on account of this behavior, just as conscientious human beings eat meat without being oppressed by any sense of guilt.

---

[96] It seems to me that in his reply 'Allamah has digressed from the main concern of the questioner and has addressed another question. Apparently what 'Allamah intends is that regardless of whether the world is temporally eternal, it is in need of God. [trans.]

As has been elucidated elsewhere, injustice in the sense of encroaching on the rights of others or of discrimination in enforcing established rules exists solely in the context of human society. As such, natural disasters do not constitute *injustice*. They may be referred to as *adversity* [*sharr*]. It should, however, be borne in mind that a natural disaster is an adversity in relation to the injured party, but in relation to the cause of the disaster, it is a good, for it is the natural effect of its cause. The disability of a six-month-old infant is an adversity, a deprivation (not injustice) caused by certain natural factors. The hardship that a dog inflicts on a cat is an inevitable adversity, not an injustice. Thus, the cat inflicts the same on a mouse.

Injustice is meaningful only in the context of human society. The human being has innumerable needs (owing to his various natural faculties and his freewill), many of which he cannot satisfy individually. For this reason, human beings come together to form societies. But for the preservation of social life, there must be a body of binding regulations that would secure, if complied with, the interests of the constituent individuals. (These interests vary, of course, depending on the social position of each individual.) In the framework of these regulations certain inalienable rights are defined for every individual.

These rights must be honored; their violation is by law forbidden. It is the violation of these contractual rights that constitutes *injustice*. So injustice is to violate another's rights: the unpleasant effects of natural elements—effects that have been arranged by the order of creation—are adversities not injustice. But in addition to natural elements, there are also instances in the context of human society that violation of an individual's rights is not injustice.

> *Curtailing an individual's rights to uphold an important truth is an adversity for the affected individual but not injustice. Similarly, the punishment inflicted on a criminal, though unpleasant*

for him, is just—
"...So should anyone aggress against you, assail him in the manner he assailed you..."[97]

In your letter,[98] you [i.e., the questioner] write, "A certain gentleman told me that a smaller animal devoured by a larger animal actually attains to a higher degree of perfection, for the flesh of the weaker animal has become part of the stronger animal. But what sort of perfection does cat meat obtains by becoming dog meat?" The concept you criticize is based on a legitimate philosophic concept, namely substantial motion [*harikat jawhari*]. It is, however, a sophisticated concept whose exposition is beyond the scope of a letter such as this.

You further state, "It is argued that God is the Owner of all things: all belongs to Him, and He has the right to do with what is His as He pleases. I realize this as well, but the issue is that the Qur'an expressly avers that God does not act unjustly." The correct explanation of this problem is as follows:

Everything in the world, including all the attributes of perfection, belongs indisputably to God. All that we enjoy, from the most insignificant to the most cherished, are blessings He has bestowed on us. He bestows these blessings without any merit on our part.

There is no greater power that could coerce Him into doing something or restrain Him from doing something. All the rights we assume for ourselves have actually been established by God. In this light, God cannot be held accountable for the adversities that befall His creatures:

---

[97] Surah al-Baqarah 2:194.

[98] Evidently, 'Allamah is replying to a long letter, which, for the sake of brevity, has been summarized in the single paragraph expressed above. [trans.]

"...God does whatever He wishes..."[99]

For, these adversities do not constitute injustice in the first place. (As such, it would be awed to think that these adversities are unjust, God being exonerated because of His status.) In other words, the pleasant things we enjoy are favors He bestows on us out of His mercy and the hardships we encounter are the suspension of these favors:

"Whatever mercy God unfolds for the people no one can withhold; and whatever He withholds no one can release, except Him..."[100]

Of course, should He confer a right on a creature, it would be an act of injustice for Him to deprive that creature of that right without a legitimate reason, and He, being Immaculate, would not commit such an injustice. For instance, to make the human being capable of attaining to felicity as the purpose of his life and existence and to promise him eternal life in Paradise and then to arbitrarily sentence him to eternal chastisement would constitute an injustice that God would not commit. In cases where human beings are condemned to eternal chastisement, it is due to their own disobedience:

"Indeed God does not wrong people in the least; rather it is people who wrong themselves."[101]

"Today no one will be done any injustice, nor will you be requited except for what you used to do."[102]

---

[99] Surah Ibrahim 14:27.

[100] Surah Fatir 35:2.

[101] Surah Yunus 10:44.

[102] Surah Ya Sin 36:54.

You further state, "They [i.e., the advocates of the doctrine of Divine justice] argue that it is the people themselves that are to blame, but what guilt could a six-month-old infant be accountable for? If his parents are guilty, why should he pay the price? If you counter that the infant will be compensated in the Hereafter, will there also be compensation for the bird that a hunter shoots down?"

It is a matter of fact that in certain cases a child is aficted with an adversity on account of his parents' guilt. But in such cases, the child's afiction is in effect the manifestation of the parents' guilt, not its punishment. As regards compensation to hunted animals, the Qur'an explicitly states that animals will also be resurrected:

> *"There is no animal on land, nor a bird that ies with its wings, but they are communities like you. We have not omitted anything from the Book. Then they will be mustered toward their Lord."*[103]

The Qur'an does not provide the details of their resurrection, but some *hadiths* state that on the Day of Judgment, God will punish horned animals for harming hornless animals. The conclusion that one draws from studying the Qur'an and the Sunnah is that there is wisdom in every phenomenon that occurs in the cosmos, whether we be aware of it or not.

In the end, you say, "The essence of my concern and the cause for my distress is that there is injustice in this world, which goes largely without requital. I am afraid that this would continue into the next world, that harmed animals would not be avenged. More fundamentally, it is wrong that there is injustice at all."

First of all, let me reiterate that most of the examples you cite are

---

[103] Surah al-An'am 6:38.

adversities not injustice, and requital is meaningful only in reference to injustice. The adversities that exist in this world have a purpose in the matrix of the order of creation. This purpose may relate to the entire system as an organic whole or to a specific part of it. But where there really is injustice, where a creature's right is violated, it will definitely be avenged; if not in this world then, as guaranteed by the Qur'an, in the Hereafter:

"...There will be no injustice today..."[104]

—"...God does not break His promise."[105]

The Question of Human Individuality and its Preservation During the Resurrection

Question

From the scientific point of view, there is no doubt that after death the human body decomposes, through a variety of natural processes, into nitrate and nitrogen, a part of this material being absorbed into the soil. These materials are then assimilated by plants, which are in turn consumed by human beings. The vegetables that people eat are converted by the body into new cells. The question is, when humans are resurrected, how will the deficiency of the bodies of former individuals be restored? If they are to be provided with the material that originally formed their bodies, then the bodies of the subsequent

---

[104] Surah al-Ghafir (or Mu'min) 40:17.
[105] Surah al-Ra'd 13:31.

humans will be left deficient, and if those materials are to remain in the bodies of the subsequent individuals, then the bodies of former individuals will be left deficient.

Answer

One should take note that science has also proven that the cells of the human body constantly undergo deterioration and change in the span of human life. So much so that every few years, the entire cells of the human body, from head to toe, are renewed, not a single cell remaining from the previous group.

Nonetheless, the human individual remains the same, not affected in any way by the rapid change his body undergoes.

To put this in clearer terms, a fifty-year-old, for instance, realizes very clearly that he is the same person as he was as an adolescent and a child; the same person has aged. The reality to which he refers as "I" (and which we term "self") has not changed. It is for this reason that if one commits a crime at a young age, he may be prosecuted for it in his later years.

Thus human individuality is actualized by one's soul, not one's body. The loss of a portion of one's bodily material does not alter one's identity. On the Day of Judgment, to whatever body the soul is reattached (whether it is his own body that has undergone change and been restored with new material or an entirely different body), it will be seen exactly as his worldly body, and he will be the same individual.

Chapter 3: Creation and Resurrection

The Purpose of Creation

Question

Does this world have a Creator? If so, what was His purpose in creating this world? Are there obligations for which we are accountable? These are questions that have puzzled the human being since time immemorial. Obviously, to answer positively to these questions would lead to more specific ones for which the human mind, due to his innate curiosity, seeks logical and definite answers. The questions mentioned above are among the most fundamental ones with which the human mind grapples. One inherently feels the need to arrive at logical and definite answers to these questions.

Answer

The reason why we inquire regarding the purpose of creation is that in doing all our personal and social activities, we strive to achieve certain goals and ideals that suit our purpose: we eat in order to satisfy our hunger; we drink water in order to quench our thirst; we dress in order to protect ourselves from harsh weather; we speak in order to convey our intentions. No human being would undertake an activity consciously without having a purpose, without the possibility of reaping some profit.

Since this is the case for us, we assume that all other intelligent creatures must follow the same logic, and thus we ask, "What is God's purpose in creation?" But is it legitimate to make this comparison? Is it always correct to extend a principle that applies to certain cases to include other cases? The answer is negative.

The only definite way to find a solution to our question would be to analyze the concept of *purpose*, for we cannot reasonably hope to solve the question through induction and by examining the innumerable cases that this question applies to.

Upon analyzing the voluntary actions we routinely perform, it becomes evident that in every case we act with the *purpose* of gaining some benefit that fulfills a need within us. In eating, for example, the purpose is to satisfy one's hunger, and once the purpose is achieved, the action is terminated. This is the case for every action we perform consciously—drinking, sitting, standing, listening, walking, etc. Even the activities that we do seemingly without any personal interest (such as the altruistic deeds that we occasionally perform) will on closer examination prove to be of some benefit, without which we would not have undertaken the activity: in all such cases we are actually fulfilling our emotional needs, relieving ourselves, for example, of the painful pity we feel for the poor.

Based on the above analysis, we may infer that, generally, the purpose of a conscious action is the drive to achieve a desired end—the fulfillment of a need—that is attainable through the action in question.

At first glance, it may appear that purposive actions are peculiar to conscious agents, which are equipped with intelligence and freewill. Paying closer attention, however, will make clear that the same properties that govern the actions of conscious agents also pertain to inanimate agents. An inanimate agent is similarly equipped with certain faculties that are responsible for satisfying its natural needs.

Thus, just as in the case of the conscious agent, the inanimate agent strives toward a particular end for the purpose of satisfying an inherent inclination. The only factor that distinguishes the conscious agent from the inanimate one is awareness: the conscious agent performs actions with awareness whereas the inanimate agent abides blindly by the dictates of its nature.

The Universal Presence of Purpose

The above elucidation clarifies, then, that purpose pervades all creatures, for the principle of cause- and-effect, which dominates the entire creation, precludes the possibility of an agent's performing an action without a purpose.

Take any individual from any species: a human being, an insect, an apple tree, a spike of wheat, a piece of iron, a molecule of oxygen; they are all similar in that they adjust to their environments and perform certain actions so as to achieve an end. Once the end is reached and the agent acquires the gain it sought, the action terminates.

This also applies in more general terms to the species collectively—such as the human species, the horse species, the apple tree species, and so on. By their peculiar activities, individuals of all species pursue certain ends in order to compensate for their inherent deficiencies and thus secure the survival of their species. And in still more general terms, this same truth applies to the entire cosmos whose various parts are, as a matter of fact, linked together in a cosmic nexus.

Generally speaking, every course of activity involves a point of origin and a point of termination. Action is an intermediary stage during which a being evolves from one state into another. Action starts when a being desires the fulfillment of a need. This desire may arise from a purely physical tendency (as in the case of natural phenomena), an instinctive drive (as in the case of animals), or a conscious decision (as in the case of human beings). The action ceases when the need is fulfilled, but this end may in turn be the starting point for another action that leads to another end.

The above explanation should suffice to demonstrate that it is inconceivable that an action should come into existence without being directed toward a definite end or that its relation with its end be fortuitous. It is just as inconceivable that an agent should initiate an action without having a causal relationship with the action and the end of the action.

Universal principles—one of which is the amazing causal order that dominates the cosmos—admit of no violation. They regulate the cosmos uniformly, rendering fortuity impossible.

According to the studies of a knowledgeable scholar, the possibility that a thing composed only of ten atoms may have come about haphazardly is one in ten billion. Therefore, to cite chance in explaining the phenomena of this world is an inane claim. The intellect, which has its roots in the Divine nature of the human being, clearly denounces such attempts at negating the necessary relation between an action, its agent, and its purpose, for such negation would destroy the very foundations of science and nullify the mind's self-evident principles.

The Cosmic Purpose

The components of this expansive universe, from the smallest particles to the most startlingly gigantic galaxies, are linked together in a true nexus, forming a uniform whole. This whole, with all its innumerable properties and modes of existence, is in motion, a general and universal motion. (This view is corroborated by philosophic arguments and scientific theories.)

The cosmos, as a uniform whole, pursues a particular goal; it is navigating toward its destination. Once that destination is reached, this ever-changing and noisy universe will be transformed into an immutable and serene world. The future world, in contrast to the present commotion, will be characterized by stability and harmony, its imperfections perfected and its potentialities actualized.

The question that this may raise is, will that stability be relative and in comparison to the present order of things? Or will it be absolute stability and serenity, free of any degree of change? The truth is that the future world will enjoy an absolute and true stability, a veritable state of perfection. The instability that is integral to the world of today will be sealed and locked away, for the world will have reached the point where it originally started out, thus completing a perfect cycle, a point whereat, to employ the "modernist" vernacular, comprehension will be four dimensional as phenomena will be free of relative temporal orientation.

What we have said above, though in brief (for, it is a very complicated subject, which we have condensed into a nutshell), makes clear that the future world toward which the cosmic caravan is navigating in full speed will be a place of perfect stability. Obviously, in attempting to digest this subject, one may encounter numerous questions, which form the material for some profound and complicated philosophic discussions (we say complicated because the topics at issue are abstract ones that fall beyond the ken of sensory perception).

From the instant we open our eyes and view the wanders of this world, all that we see is in motion, in becoming, first evolving then disintegrating. All along we have been among the passengers of this caravan, never hearing from those who leave it—"He who heard the truth was never again heard of." As such, the topic at hand is one that can be resolved solely through meticulous philosophic reasoning based on apodictic rational arguments derived from valid premises. (It should be pointed out that this philosophic topic corresponds to the religious doctrine of Resurrection as preached by Islamic religious authorities.)

God's Purpose in Creating the World

In light of what has been said above, it should be clear, then, that purpose is meaningful only when two elements are present: an agent (which strives to achieve the purpose in question in order to fulfill an inherent need) and an action (the agent's action in striving towards the purpose in question).

Furthermore, as demonstrated by sound rational arguments, God is Absolute Perfection, free of any need or imperfection. The conclusion that results from juxtaposing these two premises is that one can speak of an *end* with regard to God's action, but, in reference to the Divine Essence, it would be incorrect to speak of a purpose.

In other words, the question "What is God's purpose in creation?" can be viewed in one of two ways: if by this question, one is inquiring about the end of God's action (that is, to what end it is directed), the answer would be that our imperfect world is progressing toward a more perfect state. If, however, one means to determine what need God intends to fulfill or what benefit He desires to secure in creating the world, the question would be incorrect. [106]What our religious sources say in this regard is that God's purpose in creating the world is to benefit others not Himself.

The conclusion that results from the above analysis is that purpose is meaningful when the agent or the action has a deficiency that can be cured by achieving the purpose. For this reason, purpose, in the common definition, does not apply to beings that transcend the domain of materiality—that is, to God and the purely immaterial intellects.

However, philosophers have through meticulous analysis arrived at a more subtle understanding of purpose. They distinguish two meanings for purpose. One pertains to the action and designates its fruition; the other pertains to the agent and indicates the fulfillment of a need. It is in the first meaning that purpose is correctly applicable to the actions of immaterial beings. But to understand this, there is need for further explanation.

Actions of immaterial beings are instantaneous; that is, they do not involve motion. As such their actions constitute in and of themselves the actualization of their purpose. The same holds true with regard to the existential purpose of immaterial beings themselves. As they are perfect, their existence is in and of itself the actualization of the purpose of their existence. From this point of view, God's purpose in creating the world is solely His Essence, and the purpose of this world is to develop into the perfect world. The purpose of that perfect world would be itself: the purpose in the creation of any perfect creature is itself.

---

[106] For, it presupposes the presence of need in the Divine Essence. God, however, is Absolute Perfection; He has no need, and there is no higher perfection possible for Him to desire. [trans.]

Chapter 3: Creation and Resurrection

God's Purpose in Testing Humankind

Question

If a potter makes two vases, one with a single handle and the other with two handles, he cannot disapprove of the single-handled one for having only one handle, for it is his making. Moreover, if the vases be hidden from him, he would still know their shape, color, and other characteristics. In the case of a painter, he is fully aware of a painting once he has finished his work on it, and it would be absurd if he later claimed that he wanted to examine it to determine whether it was good or bad.

Considering these examples, let me raise the following question: God has created all celestial and terrestrial beings, all spiritual and material beings. He possesses absolute and eternal knowledge of the world, for He is the Creator and would be imperfect if He lacked such knowledge, but His Essence is Absolute Perfection. In this light, why does He need to try humankind, whom He created and whose destiny lies in His Hands?

Answer

In the Qur'an, God, the Exalted, approaches the topic of the purpose of the creation of humankind in two ways. One way is the language of the common people. In this approach, God reveals Himself as the Absolute King with absolute sovereignty, declaring that all are His slaves. When speaking in this language, He portrays this world as the preparatory stage for the next world, the Eternal World. In this preparatory stage, His slaves must comply with His commands, for which they will be rewarded in the Hereafter. In this approach, the life of this world is a test, a trial in which God is the Examiner:

"Every soul shall taste death, and We will bring upon you good and ill by way of trial..."[107]

The second approach is purely intellectual, based on the true knowledge of the world. In this approach, creation with all its good and evil is viewed as a painting, a painting that has ugly scenes as well as nice ones. From this point of view, test is meaningless. There is, however, one fundamental point that should be heeded: the spots of ink on this canvas act on their own accord. That is, they have been placed on the canvas in such a way that allows them some freedom. They should use this freedom to create pleasant scenes, but they may use it to create unpleasant ones as well. The drawings that they create will determine what future is awaiting them.

The Creation of the Heavens and Earth in Six Days

Question

God's will is actualized instantaneously. The moment He wills something, it comes into existence *ex nihilo*. Based on this truth, the question is, why did the act of creation span six days?

Answer

The above question has received sufficient attention in books of philosophy. But the problem at the heart of the question is more fundamental than what the question assumes. Material phenomena, in general, are governed by motion; everything comes about through a course of motion; creation in material phenomena is a gradual process.

---

[107] Surah al-Anbiya' 21:35.

But on the contrary, action in immaterial agents is instantaneous. So the problem is how to explain the dichotomy between the instantaneity of the cause (the immaterial agents that affect the material world) and the gradualness of the effect (the material world).

In traditional books of Islamic philosophy, this problem is referred to as "the relation of the temporal to the atemporal," or "the relation of a temporal effect to a transcendent cause." It is a very complicated discussion (you may want to refer to books of philosophy for a thorough explanation). What can be briey said in this letter is this: the concepts of gradualness, change, and time are relative concepts, similar to the concepts of small and large. These relative concepts are derived when phenomena of this world are compared to one another. In relation to God, however, all things are immutable, and such relative concepts lose their meaning. The following two verses of the Qur'an speak to this truth:

> **"All His command, when He wills something, is to say to it "Be," and it is..."**[108]

> **"Our command is but a single word, like the twinkling of an eye."**[109]

According to the former verse, what God does is solely creating [which is instantaneous], and according to the latter verse the relation of phenomena to God is beyond the scope of time; in relation to Him, all things are stable, immutable, and instantaneous.

Divine will is not an attribute of Essence; it is rather an attribute of Action, and as such is extraneous to God's Essence. In other words,

---

[108] Surah Ya Sin 36:82.

[109] Surah al-Qamar 54:50.

it applies only to the domain of Divine Activity. To say that God has willed something is to say that He has prepared the appropriate conditions for its development. (For, it must be borne in mind that the cosmos is governed by the principle of causation.) Hence, as God's will is equivalent to what is willed, in reference to instantaneous matters, the Divine will is instantaneous, and in reference to gradual matters, it is gradual.

The Effects of Belief in the Resurrection

Question

What effects can belief in Resurrection have on our character and conduct? In what ways can it inuence our social interactions? What gives rise to this question is that, as a matter of fact, human society subsists on the activities of its individuals. Human beings perform their activities out of an urge to fulfill the needs of their lives. As the human being is driven by a strong instinct of preservation, he takes pleasure in achieving whatever may be conducive to this end.

It is the life of this world that invigorates him, giving him the will to endeavor untiringly. And in this endeavor, the more he achieves his desired goals, the stronger is his enthusiasm to persist. It is this that keeps the wheels of society moving, and once it has started on the road to progress, it constantly accelerates, a newer and more profound development appearing every day. The thought of death, of the afterlife, however, brings this progress to a halt, if not paralyzing it completely.

Answer

There should be no doubt in that all heavenly religions ground their call to a great extent on human obligation and the reward of doing good. Islam, in particular, stands on three pillars, one of which is the doctrine of Resurrection. It sets this doctrine on a par with the doctrines of Divine Unity and prophethood, and as such without acknowledging this doctrine; one is not considered a Muslim. This shows clearly the importance of the doctrine of Resurrection in the framework of the Islamic faith.

The goal of Islam is to revive the primordial human nature, to bring out the pristine human nature in people. From the Islamic viewpoint, belief in Resurrection is one of the critical elements in the life of the human being, without which he is a body devoid of spirit and as such unable to attain to virtue and felicity.

Islamic doctrines and rules are not hollow conventionalities, invented to keep people busy by blindly conforming to them. They form a coherent program—composed of doctrinal, spiritual, and practical elements—which God has formulated in accordance with the inherent needs of human nature, a truth to which the following Qur'anic verses attest:

> *"O you who have faith! Answer God and the Apostle when he summons you to that which will give you life..."*[110]

> *"So set your heart on the religion as a people of pure faith, the origination of God according to which He originated mankind..."*[111]

---

[110] Surah al-Anfal 8:24.

[111] Surah al-Rum 30:30.

Thus, Islamic law is like civil law (which is the law of modern societies) in that its purpose is to provide instructions that guarantee the fulfillment of humankind's social needs as well as the needs that are critical to individual human life. Nevertheless, what differentiates the two systems is a fundamental one.

As opposed to secular civil laws, whose purview is limited to the transient and material life of this world and which are rooted in the sentiments of the majority, the heavenly faith of Islam takes into account the eternal life of the human being, which extends beyond death. In this outlook, one's felicity and misery in the Hereafter are directly related to one's conduct in this world. Thus, Islam offers a program that is based on intellectuality, not sentimentality.

From the point of view of modern civil law, the will of the majority is binding. But according to Islam, only those regulations that are true and verifiable by the intellect are enforceable, irrespective of their agreement with the sentiments of the majority.

Islam declares that the pristine human being, unadulterated by superstition and egotism, recognizes through his primordial nature the reality of Resurrection and, consequently, his eternal life. Unlike the material human being—who is utterly oblivious of his Origin and End, blindly follows his brute instincts, and desires only to indulge his material appetites—the pristine human being acknowledges that he must live in compliance with his intellect (a special grace conferred exclusively unto humankind), always cognizant of what it requires of him.

For the pristine human being, belief in the Day of Judgment and Resurrection affects every social and individual aspect of life: intellectual, moral, and spiritual. It affects one's intellectual life by shedding light on the true state of the soul and all other phenomena. In this light, one finds oneself as a limited and insignificant particle in the universe, which is journeying like a caravan, day and night, toward the everlasting world.

In other words, one finds oneself relentlessly propelled from one side by the Hand of Creation (the Efficient Cause) and attracted from the other side by the End of Creation (the Resurrection). This insight in one's intellectual outlook in turn inuences one's moral and spiritual state. Seeing the true state of things, one then restrains one's sentiments and desires so as to traverse this path in a manner appropriate to the True End.

When the human being considers how his needs make him dependent on the various parts of this restless world and how he, like a blade of hay, is thrust to and fro in the turbulent sea of the cosmos, moving ever closer to the Cosmic End, he will no longer indulge in selfish, pompous, and ignorant self-displays, he will no longer engage in the futile toils of this material world—which turn people into machines—more than what is necessary for a eeting life. This attitude elevates the human being beyond the personal and social strife, relieving him of the many exacting but vain burdens that erode his true life.

One so enlightened knows that, should he relinquish his eeting life in the way of virtue, he will have instead an eternal life in felicity, enjoying the rewards of his good deeds. As such, there is no need to instill in his mind the various superstitions that are so prevalent today to persuade him to make sacrifices.

Secular societies, however, resort to illusory ideals in order to compel their people to make sacrifices. They invoke, say, the "sanctities of society:" liberty, law, and patriotism. They encourage their people to secure an honorable name that would go down in history, thus acquiring, so they say, an "eternal life." The truth, however, is that if death is annihilation, as the materialists contend, all these so-called ideals are vain superstitions.

Among the spiritual advantages of having belief in the Hereafter is that it constantly invigorates the soul, for one knows that there will be a day when oppression will be avenged and all rights redeemed, a day when virtuous deeds will be appreciated—a most lofty appreciation. But its main effect is the spirit of vigilance it instills in one's spirit: one is aware that one's actions, whether public or private, are being watched by the All-knowing, the All-seeing God and that there is a day ahead when He will scrutinize one's deeds with the greatest attention. This belief restrains one such that no undercover police could ever achieve, for police is an outward restraint, whereas this belief is an inward guard from which nothing can be concealed.

The above explanation makes clear that the allegation that belief in an afterlife undercuts a society's motivation for work and progress is invalid. Motivation is a state of mind engendered by a sense of need, and belief in the Hereafter only serves to accentuate this sense.

This truth is historically demonstrable. Looking back at the early period of Islam, when Muslims were more firm in their faith, we see that social advancement was astonishing; Muslims have never again been able to regain that vigor. Of course, belief in the Hereafter does reduce one's preoccupation with sensuality; it does preclude people from putting their lives on the line for nonsensical and illusory concerns.

Chapter 4: Miscellaneous Questions

The Question of Gender Equality in Islam and Women's Participation in Politics

Question

Does Islamic law consider man and woman equal? And does Islam allow women to engage in politics and governmental affairs on a par with men?

Answer

Before the advent of Islam, societies took one of two positions concerning women. Some societies treated women as domestic animals. They did not count women as members of the society; women were exploited for the benefit of the society, that is, the men. In the more civilized societies, women were second-class citizens, comparable to minors and slaves. In these societies, women had some limited rights that were strictly controlled by men. But Islam, for the first time in the history of humankind, acknowledged women's full membership in the society, appreciating their efforts as equal to those of men:

> *"...I [God] do not waste the work of any worker among you, whether male or female..."*[112]

There are only three areas in which Islam forbids women's participation: leadership[113], judicature, and warfare (i.e., participation in combat; otherwise, women may engage in other affairs related to war). The logic behind this difference, to the extent that we can infer from Islamic sources, is that women are more sentimental than men. The three areas mentioned above should be handled only with recourse to reason, and as such men are better qualified in them.

The most persuasive evidence in support of this position is the failure of the efforts of Western countries—which have advocated similar education for both genders—to train a substantial number of female professionals in these three areas. In the record of the prominent figures in these three areas, women historically hold a negligible share (as opposed to such areas as nursing, dancing, acting, painting, and music in which women excel).

The Question of Inheritance

---

[112] Surah Al 'Imran 3:195.

[113] That is, acting as the head of state; but, other governmental positions are open to women. [trans.]

Question

Why does the woman inherit less than the man in Islamic law?

Answer

In Islam, the woman takes one-third of the inheritance and the man two-thirds. The reason for this difference, as stated by a *hadith*, is that it is the man's duty to take care of the expenses of the family, including the woman. The latter rule in turn is based on man's peculiar nature, as he is less sentimental than she.

Let me give a more thorough explanation. When one generation passes away, the wealth is inherited by the next generation. According to Islamic law, of this wealth, two-thirds goes to men and one-third to women. The two-thirds portion that men inherit must be spent for the welfare of the entire family, whereas women have no obligation to share their one-third.

Consequently, although men are put in charge of two-thirds of the wealth, it is women who actually enjoy two-thirds of the wealth [by holding on to their one-third and at the same time benefitting from the two-thirds that goes to men]. This is the fairest possible distribution of wealth—not to mention the positive effects that such a distribution has in maintaining the family unit (as will be elaborated below).

The Question of Divorce

Question

Why is divorce a prerogative of the man?

Answer

Once again this seems to be, as can be inferred from Islamic sources, due to the natural difference between the two genders. Nevertheless, Islamic law offers the woman the right at the time of marriage to limit her spouse's rights and to define for herself certain means to obtain divorce.

The Woman's Financial Independence

Question

Does Islamic law allow women to engage in financial activities independently?

Answer

In Islam women have complete freedom in their financial activities.

The Question of Polygamy in Islam

Question

Why does Islam allow men to have more than one spouse?

Answer

It is common knowledge that Islam does not enforce polygamy; rather, it only permits a man to marry up to four wives provided he treats all fairly. There are a number of factors on which this permission is contingent. One general condition is that polygamy should not lead to social imbalance by causing a shortage of marriageable women. Moreover, men are obliged to provide their family with suitable residence and appropriate clothing and food. Considering the above two qualifications makes clear that there are only a very small number of men eligible to have multiple wives.

Of course, it should not escape our attention that normally, due to various factors, there is a surplus of marriageable women. The normal life span of women is longer than that of men, and there are normally more widows than widowers (especially taking into account that fatal casualties are more frequent in men than in women). Recently newspapers and magazines reported that German women have been petitioning the government to implement a marriage law that would allow for men to have more than one wife. But the government, under pressure from the Vatican, has so far rejected their petition.

Furthermore, it should be noted that women's prevalent aversion to polygamy is not innate, otherwise how could there be so many women from various cultures who are bound in polygamous marriages and are happy and satisfied with their life.[114]

Islam, the Perfect Religion

Question

It is a matter of fact that Islam has failed to keep up with the times. This has rendered it incompatible with modern life. I don't see how anyone could reasonably deny this truth.

---

[114] That is, women's aversion to polygamy, which is more prevalent in Western countries, is not due to an inherent tendency; it rather results from certain cultural factors present in some—not all—regions. [trans.]

Answer

To say that Islam is incompatible with modern life is nonsense. The passing of time does not bring about any substantial change that would necessitate a fundamental alteration of social law; night and day are the same; our planet has remained unchanged for millennia. What has changed is humankind's increasing expectations and needs as the result of the rapid progress of technology. The pleasures that kings of the past could not dream of are being sought by today's poor. This change in the social mood is similar to the change of mood that an individual undergoes in response to varying circumstances.

Let me illustrate this by a simple example. An impoverished person strives primarily to satisfy his hunger. Once he has enough food, he starts worrying about his clothing. And when that is solved, he makes plans to buy a house, marry, and have children. Then, he strives to increase his wealth, acquire fame, and indulge himself with as many entertainments as he can manage.

Laws of modern civilized societies are based on (or so it is claimed) the will of the majority, even when what they will is harmful to them; the majority disregards the minority will, even if it is in the interests of the entire society. Islam, however, takes a different position. In its law, Islam sets the primordial human nature as the criterion. Islamic law is based on the human being's peculiar constitution and the various faculties embedded therein. Thus, Islam seeks to secure the real interests of humankind, irrespective of the will of the majority. It is such a law that Islam decrees as the *shari'ah*.

The *shari'ah* is not susceptible to change, for it is based on the human being's immutable nature. Of course, in addition to its unchanging law, the *shari'ah*, Islam allows for certain temporary regulations to accommodate the changing conditions of human society.

The relation of these temporary regulations to the *shari'ah* is analogous to the relation of statutes established by a state's parliament, which can be revoked, to its constitution, which is permanent and irrevocable. Thus Islamic law authorizes the Islamic head of state to enact, within the framework of the *shari'ah*, regulations necessary for meeting the needs caused by various circumstances. But as soon as those circumstances change, the regulations decreed to accommodate them automatically expire, while the *shari'ah* remains intact.

Based on the abovementioned, Islamic law has two sets of rules. One set comprises those rules that are based on the immutable human nature and is designated as the *shari'ah*; the other consists of temporary regulations enacted by the Islamic head of state in response to various circumstances. An example of the latter is the body of regulations required to secure safe transportation, regulations that were unnecessary before modern means of transportation were invented.

Islam's Agreement with the Primordial Human Nature

Question

Wouldn't you agree that many of the regulations that were established in the early years of Islam, over 1400 years ago, need to be modified?

Answer

In this regard see the answer to the previous question. I will once again underscore that the basis of Islamic law is human nature not the whim of the majority. God, the Exalted, says:

"Set your heart on the religion as a people of pure faith, the origina-

tion of God, according to which He originated humankind. There is no alteration in God's creation."[115]

The Question of Zaynab's Leadership

Question

Can it not be argued that Zaynab was the crown princess? If so, this is sufficient evidence that Islam sets no limitation on women's social activities, and those of them who are qualified can advance alongside men.

Answer

There is no evidence to support this claim. Moreover, there are no such titles as prince and princess in Islam. If by princess you mean the successor to the previous *imam*, your assumption is invalid. It is beyond doubt that based on definitive historical sources, the successor of the Third Imam was his son, 'Ali ibn al-Husayn, not Lady Zaynab. It is, however, true that she participated in Imam al-Husayn's movement in fighting Yazid's oppression. Imam al-Husayn entrusted to his sister heavy obligations that demanded a high level of knowledge and a strong will. Her success in fulfilling them proved her amazing spiritual strength.

But let us address the crux of your concern, the question of gender equality. Fundamentally, Islam acknowledges only two factors for superiority: knowledge and piety. God, the Exalted, states this in His Book:

---

[115] Surah al-Rum 30:30.

"...Indeed the noblest of you in the sight of God is the most Godwary among you..."[116]

"...Are those who know equal to those who do not know..."[117]

Other such factors as gender, wealth, high birth, and popularity, which other cultures may look upon as tokens of superiority, hold no real value. Thus, Muslim women can compete with and even surpass men in every field (bearing in mind, of course, that they cannot serve as head of state, act as judge, or participate in combat).

The Islamic Perspective on Family

Question

What is Islam's view concerning the institutions of marriage and family?

Answer

A detailed explanation regarding Islam's perspective on marriage, family, and the general principles that govern familial relationships is beyond the scope of this letter. However, I will very briey touch on some of the important topics.

Islam recognizes marriage as the fundamental building block in the formation and the preservation of society. In order to organize humankind into societies, the Hand of Creation has split the human species into two genders, implanting in each gender an instinctive

---

[116] Surah al-Hujurat 49: 13.

[117] Surah al-Zumar 39:9.

gravitation toward the other. The lowest manifestation of this mutual gravitation is the presence of distinctive sexual organs in the two. It is this mutual gravitation that brings the two genders together to beget children.

Out of this union a child is born whose substance derives from both parents. Due to the intense affection the parents feel toward this creature, they endure the pains of child birth and the hardships involved in rearing it. These difficulties savored by the accompanying emotional pleasure only serve to strengthen the emotional bond between the parents and the child, and this in turn invigorates the parents to multiply their efforts in training their child. These parental emotions, in return, attach the child ever more strongly to his parents. Thus, the family is forged—the building block from which cities and nations are constructed.

It is obvious that in order to preserve the society, the instinctive sexual drive must be curbed. The way to achieve this is by confining each gender's sexual gratification to its formal partner from the opposite gender. This will ensure that the father of every child is identified (the mother, of course, is not in need of such a measure, as her pregnancy is the clearest mark that she is the mother of the infant she is bearing). Without such a formal arrangement to curb the sexual gratification of the two genders, young adults would seldom agree to suffer the hardships of forming a family. Absence of formal families would lead to uncertainty in determining the real fathers of children born into the society.

This uncertainty will in turn weaken the emotional bond between the parents and the children, which is the fabric that holds the family together. In time, the prevalence of fornication in society—in addition to the numerous hygienic, social, and moral problems that such unrestrained sexual relations engender—will utterly destroy family affections, a fact already evident in countries where sexual relations are given free rein—a trend that threatens the survival of humankind. An article I read some years ago reported that annually three hundred thousand infants are born to single mothers in the United States as the result of promiscuous intercourse done in the heat of the moment and without prior engagement.

Hence, Islam forbids sexual gratification between the two genders outside the institution of marriage and makes the expenses of rearing the child a responsibility of the father as the child's guardian. In addition, Islam prohibits marriage between family relations who have frequent contact with one another. Thus, it is considered incestuous for a man to marry his mother, sister, aunt, or niece. The following are other females whom a man is prohibited to marry: daughter-in-law, mother-in-law, stepdaughter (if he has had intercourse with the stepdaughter's mother), sister-in-law (as long as her sister is married to the man in question), and women married to other men. The same rule applies to the relations-by- suckling.[118]

(All of the rules mentioned here are derived from the Qur'an and the tradition of the Noble Prophet and the Imams as recorded in books of *hadith*.)

The Question of Divorce

Question

How does Islam view divorce?

---

[118] In Islamic law, when a child is suckled by a woman other than her mother, the woman is legally her second mother and her children the siblings of the suckling. As such, the same marriage rules that apply to one's real mother and siblings apply to one's mother- and siblings-by-suckling. [trans.]

Answer

Islamic law does sanction divorce but only as a last resort for terminating a miserable conjugal relationship plagued by disagreement. This is one of the distinctions that prove Islam's superiority to all other faiths. Islam sanctioned divorce centuries before Western "civilized" countries realized its necessity.

Women's Right in Choosing their Spouse

Question

Does Islam grant women the right to choose their spouse freely?

Answer

Islamic law requires the wholehearted consent of the woman for the validity of a marriage contract. Thus according to Islam, women are free in choosing their spouse.

Children Being in the Custody of Men

Question

In the event of a divorce, to which party does Islamic law grant the custody of children?

Answer

Divorcees have the right to keep the children up to the age of seven, but even if the children remain with their mothers, the male guardian is in charge of paying their expenses. (To explicate the reasoning for this rule is beyond the scope of this letter; you may refer to the corpus of Islamic jurisprudence to find the reasoning.)[119]

A Saying from 'Ali

Question

It is reported that Imam 'Ali said that parents must train their children with an eye to the future? If this report is correct, one can extrapolate that Islamic regulations should also be modified to make them compatible with the changing circumstances of time and place?

Answer

First of all, it should be noted that this saying is attributed to Imam 'Ali in *"Nahj al-Balaghah"* with a discontinuous chain of transmission.[120] Assuming that it is authentic, the meaning appears to be that we should refrain from imposing on our children the habits and customs with which we were raised, for it will constrain their imagination and innovativeness, consequently hindering their capacity for progress. If in our time, horses and donkeys were means of transportation, we

---

[119] I must reexamine what comes before this point (the first part of this chapter and the previous chapters) to make sure that subjunctives are used correctly. [note]

[120] A discontinuous chain of transmission is one in which one or more transmitters are lacking. In the science of hadithology ['ilm al-dirayah] such a chain of transmission is considered a defect that reduces the possibility of it's being authentic. [trans.]

should not force our children to use the same.

The saying, however, is not in reference to Islamic law (whose irrevocability is explicitly affirmed by the Qur'an and the Sunnah); if it were, it would be inacceptable as it would contravene the Qur'an, which affirms the permanence of the *shari'ah*. (There are numerous *hadith*s narrated from the Imams that state that *hadith*s must be dismissed as unauthentic if they contradict the Qur'an.)

The Irrevocability of the Shari'ah

Question

Why have religious authorities of Islam neglected modifying Islamic law to make it compatible with changing circumstances of the times?

Answer

Religious authorities have no right to change the Divine law as embodied by the *shari'ah*. Their authority is limited to arriving at the secondary rules of Islam on the basis of the Qur'an and the Sunnah, similar to the lawyer whose function is merely to infer legal arguments from his country's legal code; he does not have the right to alter the country's constitution. Likewise, in Islam religious authorities, including the Imams whom are entrusted with teaching the *shari'ah*—and even the Prophet, for that matter—have no right to alter the *shari'ah* at their own discretion.

Such questions as the ones posed here stem from the mindset dominant in Western societies, which depicts Divine prophets merely as gifted individuals and social reformers who rose up to secure the rights of their people and to help them advance. Scholars with this mindset explain that these social reformers had to establish certain rules to meet the needs of their times.

Thus, they conclude, the rules instituted by these so-called prophets were the product of their own thought, not divine revelation. But in order to convince people to follow their instructions, they had to introduce themselves as prophets sent by God with a revealed book (which was actually their own work).

If we accept this account, then, we would obviously be obliged to agree that religious law must change so as to meet the needs of every age. This account, however, is wrong. Those who put forth such an account have failed to conduct a thorough study of the teachings of Divine prophets, grounding their analysis solely on unfounded conjectures. The Noble Qur'an and the definitive *hadiths* narrated from the Prophet (we do not take into account the sacred books of previous religions, as they have been distorted) disprove this account.

I will express a few points very briey from the Qur'an and the Sunnah:

1. The Qur'an explicitly states that the Prophet has no right to make changes to the Revelation as he receives it, for he is only a messenger (see *Surah al-Ma'idah* 5:92 and 99).
2. The Qur'an asserts that Islam is not a product of human intelligence; it is rather the embodiment of the instructions that God has revealed to His Prophet (see *Surah al-Haqqah* 69:40-43).
3. In reply to those who accused the Prophet of attributing his own thoughts to God, the Qur'an affirms that it is the veritable word of God, and as such its content cannot be the product of the human mind (see *Surah al-Muddathir* 69:25).
4. The Qur'an expressly announces that Muhammad is the Final Prophet and the Qur'an the final Revelation, and hence the content of the Qur'an is valid for all time (see *Surah al-Ahzab* 33:40).

The Question of Islam's Conflict with Modern Science and Technology

Question

How can you deny that Islam's falling into disfavor with the youth is due to its backward principles, which are incompatible with modern science and technology?

Answer

We would have preferred you mentioned a few examples of the "backward principles" of Islam so that we could have replied with appropriate arguments. There are no "backward principles" in Islam, though there are many backward Muslims. Divine religions, in general, and Islam, in particular, pertain to the eternal life, to humankind's connection with the supra-natural. How could this conflict be in any way related to modern science and technology per se? Modern science and technology deal with material phenomena and are thus irrelevant to matters that transcend materiality.

The reason why some Muslim youths turn away from Islam is not a fault on the part of Islam. This is evidenced by noting that this trend extends beyond Islam, encompassing even those universal principles that derive from human conscience and spirituality.

The prevalence of hypocrisy, sexual promiscuity, and libertinism among educated Muslim youths is proof that they despise truth and virtue altogether, not only Islam. Nonetheless, there are a good number of educated Muslim youths who have embellished their souls with virtue and who remain obedient to the so-called backward Islamic principles. They see no conflict between Islam and modern science and technology and feel no dissatisfaction with their lives as believers. Thus, parents and those responsible for the country's culture are to blame for the youth's discontent with Islam. Islam embodies morality and virtue.

Men's Deserving Equal Blame for Indecent Acts

Question

Why is it that in immoral sexual acts, for which the male and the female parties are equally responsible, women receive a harsher treatment? If Islam considers men stronger, then they should be better able to rein in their desires, and so when they violate the bounds of modesty, they should deserve a more severe punishment.

Answer

As regards the degree of responsibility in an immoral sexual act, Islam does not discriminate between the two genders.

A False Contention

Question

It is well-known that the Prophet strongly advised foster parents to treat their adopted children as they treat their real children. Why, then, did he wish to marry his foster son's ex-wife?

Answer

In Islam, the relationship between foster children and foster parents is not governed by the same regulations that pertain to real children. The account you mention is historically incorrect. It is a false story fabricated by Islam's opponents, especially some Christians of the West.

The Prophet married Zayd's divorced wife to publically demonstrate the invalidity of the long-standing pre-Islamic tradition of Arabia, according to which adopted children were treated as real children. This tradition had given rise to the practice of trading children among families. (This issue is mentioned in *Surah al-Ahzab*.)

The Prophet's Marriage in old Age with Young 'A'ishah

Question

It is hard to understand why the Prophet, a role model for all humanity, married, in old age, 'A'ishah—a girl of nine years.

Answer

There are two problems that may result from the marriage of an old man with a young girl. First, the girl may not enjoy having sex with a man so much older than she. Second, due to the great age difference, the husband will in all likelihood die before his wife, leaving her widowed. Although these two problems may render such a marriage undesirable, there, nevertheless, may exist more important reasons that would make it viable.

One with a minimum knowledge of Islamic history would agree

that the Prophet was no epicurean. His actions were based on reason, not sentiment. Thus, this marriage can be construed as the Prophet's attempt to demonstrate that age is not a condition in marriage. In addition, this marriage was advantageous to the Prophet's ministry.

Let me also add that older men are not necessarily unattractive. A few years ago, at the time of Eisenhower's presidency, one of the popular magazines of the United States conducted a poll, in which single women were asked to choose their favorite man. Eisenhower turned out to be the most popular, though he was neither young nor particularly handsome.

Legality of Temporary Marriage in Islam

Question

What is your opinion concerning temporary marriage, which the Sunnis condemn? Is it not a violation of human rights—objectifying women as means for the gratification of men?

Answer

The legality of temporary marriage is affirmed by the *Surah al-Nisa'* 4:24, and thus the Shi'ahs do not mind the opposition of the Sunnis on this issue. Temporary marriage is sanctioned by the Qur'an; it was practiced during the Prophet's lifetime, the caliphate of the First Caliph, and part of that of the Second Caliph. The latter, however, decided to ban temporary marriage. But it should go without saying that rules established by the Qur'an can be rescinded only by the Qur'an; the rules of the *shari'ah* are beyond the authority of the Islamic ruler.

There is, in addition, a different line of reasoning that vindicates temporary marriage, and it is by heeding the rationale for the legality of divorce. From a jurisprudential point of view, the legality of divorce is evidence that marriage can be temporary. (Of course, in practicing temporary marriage, the parties engaged should be cognizant of the possible problems that this contract could entail.)

Let me turn to the point about female objectification; this claim is unfounded. The female party enters into this relationship of her own accord and enjoys the same benefits and pleasures as the male party; if it is companionship, pleasure, or having children that they seek, it is a benefit for both. As such, in this relationship neither party is victimized.

Moreover, an examination of various societies will show that sexual relations are not limited to permanent marriage. The reason is that there are cases where a person's legitimate sexual needs cannot—for various reasons—be fulfilled through permanent marriage. And for this very obvious reason, there is no government that could claim to have confined sexual relations to temporary marriage and completely eliminated fornication.

Governments must inevitably accommodate for some sort of temporary marriage so as to avoid the negative consequences of fornication while also fully satisfying their constituents' natural sexual needs. The Master of the Faithful, Imam 'Ali, once said, "If the Second Caliph had not banned temporary marriage, only he who is doomed to damnation would commit fornication."

I would also like to make a point concerning the questioner's reference to "human rights." My assumption is that the questioner is not alluding to human rights as treated by the ancient laws of Rome and Hammurabi, which equated women with animals or, in more humane cases, slaves; rather, he is referring to the Western "human rights."

It is unfortunate that we tend to think of the Western society as the epitome of human civilization and of Western people as perfect examples of humanity. These societies, which are assumed to be the crown of all societies, should be examined more closely. What do they practice in lieu of the "inhuman" temporary marriage? How do men and woman interact in these "most civilized" societies? How do they confront cases where permanent marriage is not the solution? For the answer, one only needs to read the disturbing statistics published in this regard.

Weakness of Muslims not due to Islam

Question

Westerners contend that Islam is a religion suitable only to primitive societies, to rural communities, to nomads, and, generally speaking, to all those who have failed to keep up with the advanced modern civilization. As is evident, not a single Muslim nation is among the technologically advanced. Why is this? Could Islamic principles be reformed to become acceptable to the intelligentsia and consistent with modern science?

Answer

Indeed, Muslim countries are not among the advanced countries. But, the question is, in which of these countries is Islam really observed? Carrying the name of Islam is one thing, practicing it another. Other than a few private rituals that Muslims perform as a habit—prayer, fasting, and *hajj*—are Islam's social and legal laws observed? No! So how can the weakness of Muslims be blamed on Islam?

One may contend that if Islam was a progressive ideology and its principles conducive to social progress, it would have enjoyed popularity and would not have been forsaken as it is today. But a look at the state of liberal democracy will disprove this contention. Communism has for many years now resisted the incursion of liberal democracy.

Not only that, it has assailed liberal democracy in its very stronghold—Europe and America—bringing under its sway nearly half of the global population. And communism has achieved all this in less than half a century since its inception. Now, is it legitimate to invoke this truth to claim that communism is progressive and liberal democracy backward?[121]

Furthermore, decadence has beset not only Muslim lands; all Asian and African countries—whether Hindu, Buddhist, Christian, or Muslim—are in a similar state of decadence. The fault of Asian and African countries, which are rich in natural resources, is their being besieged by the West's insatiable appetite; they are at once the endless reservoir from which the West derives its raw materials and the market into which it pours its myriad products. Their populations, Muslim or otherwise, are slaves for Western masters, and though they change the pretexts under which they dominate Eastern countries, they will always view Easterners as their slaves. And so, as long as Eastern countries remain obedient slaves to the West, they will never advance.

As regards the second part of your question (could Islamic principles be reformed to become acceptable to the intelligentsia and consistent with modern science?), let it be said that Islamic principles, as embodied by the Qur'an and the Sunnah, are—as these sources themselves affirm—immutable and unalterable. Islam, as the true religion, is the

---

[121] Although the example that 'Allamah cites is no longer existent, the essence of this comparison is nonetheless true. What 'Allamah is arguing for is that the rise and fall in the popularity of an ideology is no evidence, for or against, its truth. The Earth was round even when Galileo was persecuted for saying so. As such, even if Islam were unpopular, that would not make Islam any less true. [trans.]

straight path, whether the intelligentsia find it palatable or not. It is they who are in need of embracing the truth; [the truth cannot bend itself to gratify their vainglory]. God, the Exalted, says,

> "There is no compulsion in religion: rectitude has become distinct from error..."[122]

(I would have preferred to hear concrete examples of Islamic principles that you [the questioner] claim are in conict with modern science.)

Equal Treatment for All in Islamic Law

Question

The Prophet and Imam 'Ali both affirmed that a person's worth is determined by his conduct, not by family or ethnic ties. Why, then, do the Shi'ahs pay special respect to the progeny of 'Ali and Muhammad?

Answer

In Islam all are equal before justice, whether king or peasant, rich or poor, strong or weak, man or woman, white or black; in this respect even the Prophet and the Imams are equal in relation to all others. Such biases and privileges should not be grounds to give some more than their share or deprive others of their rights. This holds even when dealing with the Prophet's offspring.

> *Nonetheless, the Shi'ahs pay special respect to the Prophet's progeny in compliance with the Qur'an:*

---

[122] Surah al-Baqarah 2:256.

"...Say, 'I do not ask of you any reward...except the affection for the Relatives.'"[123]

The reason why the Qur'an demands that the faithful hold the Prophet's household in high esteem became manifest when he passed away. His children received such cruel treatment as the children of no previous prophet had ever experienced. For centuries, his children lived under the harshest circumstances. They were frequently tortured for long periods in dark dungeons, beheaded, buried alive, and poisoned. After gaining relative peace and independence, the Shi'ahs sought to make up for the cruelties that the Prophet's progeny had undergone at the hands of the supposedly Muslim rulers.

The Reason why Consumption of Pork is Prohibited by Islamic Law

Question

Why does Islam prohibit consumption of pork?

---

[123] Surah al-Shawra 42:23; "the Relatives": the Prophet's household as clarified by verse 33 of Surah al-Ahzab:"purify Indeed God has willed to purge you, O People of the Household, of all impurity and to you—a thorough purification." This phrase is in reference to 'Ali, Fatimah, al-Hasan, and al-Husayn ("the Relatives" as mentioned in 42:23). This reading is unambiguously indicated by the sudden change in tone, which separates this phrase from what comes before and what follows. In his Qur'anic commentary, Jalal al-Din al-Suyuti—the highly esteemed Sunni scholar—provides a number of traditions that confirm the reading presented here of the two verses in question; see Jalal al-Din al-Suyuti, Al-Durr al- Manthur (Dar al-Ma'rifah: Beirut), vol. 5, pp. 198-9 and vol. 6, p. 7. [trans.]

Answer

It is not only Islam that prohibits eating pork. As the Evangel and the Torah indicate, eating pork was prohibited in the dietary laws of previous religions as well. The reason commonly expressed for this prohibition is that pork is harmful for one's physical and spiritual health, for it feeds on canonically unclean materials.

The Reason why Consumption of Alcoholic Beverages is Prohibited by Islam

Question

Why does Islam forbid the consumption of alcoholic beverages?

Answer

Islam considers rationality the differentia that sets humankind above all other animals and the foundation of knowledge. Obviously, intoxicants, including alcoholic beverages, undermine this defining human quality. Alcoholic beverages are responsible, at least partially, for various crimes, transgressions, and the prevalent immorality. In addition, alcohol causes physical and mental damage and entails adverse hereditary effects. This is what the Qur'an says in this regard:

> "O you who have faith! Indeed wine, gambling, idols, and the divining arrows are an abomination of Satan's doing, so avoid them, so that you may be felicitous. Indeed Satan seeks to cast enmity and hatred among you through wine and gambling, and to hinder you from the remembrance of

God and from prayer. Will you, then, relinquish?"[124]

Islam's Restrictions on Sexual Relations

Question

How does Islam view love and sexual relations?

Answer

Intimate relations (intercourse or actions that may lead to that end) between the two sexes are forbidden outside marriage. The reason for this prohibition is not the possibility that such extramarital relations may infringe on the rights of one of the two parties—as is the purported basis for the limitations established by laws of democratic states. Indeed, if this was the reason, it could have been argued that mutual consent of the two parties involved would render such a relationship legitimate.

This limitation is based on considerations concerning the wellbeing of the society and the importance of identifying the fathers of children born into a society. On the basis of these considerations, all types of fornication are illegitimate. It is on account of these same social concerns that Islamic law considers homosexuality a crime.[125]

---

[124] Surah al-Ma'idah 5:90-91

[125] It should be noted that in this answer, 'Allamah approaches the question from a strictly legal standpoint. Otherwise, there are also moral and spiritual grounds for the restrictions Islam imposes on sexual relations. [trans.]

The Irrevocability of Islamic Law

Question

What is your opinion regarding the question of reform in Islamic law? If you consider reform possible, shouldn't religious authorities take the lead? Or are they waiting for the reform to happen and then to passively acquiesce?

Answer

I have given a thorough explanation regarding this question in previous chapters, thus I will only briey summarize what I have said there. The *shari'ah*, the irrevocable law from God, is timeless. Religious authorities have no right to take the lead or to follow others. In this regard, God speaks the following words to the Noble Prophet:

> *"Had We not fortified you, certainly you might have inclined toward [the pagans] a bit. Then We would have surely made you taste a double punishment in this life and a double punishment after death, and then you would have not found for yourself any helper against Us."*[126]

The Qur'an and the Sunnah: The only Sources of Islamic Doctrine

---

[126] Surah Isra' 17:74-75.

Question

Do you have absolute faith in every Islamic doctrine and rule? Do you ever consider the possibility that they may be invalid?

Answer

Any doctrine or rule that is not derived from the Qur'an or the Sunnah is unwarranted. The articles of the *shari'ah*, however, are beyond doubt. They are based on definitive sources. Thus it is impermissible to violate them on the pretext of their being doubtful.

Explaining a Saying of Imam 'Ali

Question

There is a saying of Imam 'Ali to the effect that we should not be Muslim on account of our parents' being Muslim. We should believe only that which we can reasonably accept. Considering this saying, don't you think that every individual should be allowed to accept those Islamic principles that he finds reasonable and put aside those of which he is not convinced?

Answer

The saying in question is in reference to the principal religious doctrines, which one must accept through rational reasoning. It does not pertain to religious law, which the believer must accept on faith; he cannot select certain rules and reject others. All legal systems require this cohesion, and so it is not peculiar to Islam. When an authority enforces a law, it is taken for granted that all the rules included are binding.

Allowing people to select from the rules those they find desirable will inevitably lead to the dissolution of law. Thus, even so-called democratic constitutions do not permit such freedom.

Furthermore, when one affirms Islam's principal doctrines, one is implicitly agreeing that all Islamic rules are from God, and He is unerring. The purpose of the rules He has established is to secure the true interests of humankind. The acknowledgment of this truth will lead to unquestioning faith, even in relation to the rules whose logic one is ignorant of.

Islam, the True Religion from God

Question

Following on the previous question, the saying could also be read to indicate that every individual is free to choose the religion he finds agreeable?

Answer

Religion, in general, consists of a belief system regarding the world and the human being and a set of practices whose function is to ensure the conformity of the believer's conduct with the belief system. Religion is not a diversion that one could choose whimsically. It is, rather, a truth to which one must conform, though voluntarily. To make this tangible, let me cite an analogy.

It is a matter of fact that the Sun is the luminous source that enlightens the day. Are we free to express every illusion that may pass our mind regarding the Sun as a scientific theory? Obviously, we have no such liberty. The correct approach is to acknowledge the truth and make our life conform to it. Thus, if the saying in question, coming from a religious authority of Islam, really meant that people were free to choose whichever religion they pleased, it would have been a sign that Islam was a false religion.

The Qur'an as the authoritative source of Islamic doctrine says the following in regard to this question:

> *"Indeed with God, the [true] religion is Islam..."*[127]
>
> *"Should anyone follow a religion other than Islam, it shall never be accepted from him, and he will be among the losers in the Hereafter..."*[128]

From the various religions that exist around the world, Islam grants recognition only to three: Christianity, Judaism, and Zoroastrianism. But what this recognition means—as may be inferred from the Qur'an—is that their adherents may maintain their religion in an Islamic state without being forced to convert to Islam, not that these religions are valid.

The Crescent as the Symbol of Islam

Question

Why does the crescent represent Islam?

---

[127] Surah Al 'Imran 3:19.

[128] Surah Al 'Imran 3:85.

Answer

In Islam there is no such symbol as the crescent. The star and the crescent came into widespread use as the symbol of Islam following the Crusades to oppose the Christian symbol of the Cross, and the ags of most Muslim countries now incorporate this symbol.

Voyage to the Moon from the Perspective of Islam

Question

What is your opinion concerning the voyage to the moon, which will be possible for humankind in the near future?

Answer

There is not a particular Islamic point of view concerning the voyage to the moon. What can, however, be said in this regard is that in Islam the planets and stars, with the amazing order that governs their motion, are viewed as evidence of the One, Wise God, who has created everything there is in the universe for the sake of the human being.

The Role of Arabic Language in Islamic Culture

Question

Why has Arabic been placed among the requirements of faith such that Muslims are obliged to recite the Qur'an, the prayers and other rituals in Arabic?

Answer

The reason Muslims are obliged to learn the Qur'an in its original language is that the Qur'an is a miracle in its literature as well as in its meaning. Moreover, Islam requires that the words of the prayer be uttered in Arabic. In addition, the main sources of Islam—the Qur'an and the *hadiths* passed down from the Prophet and the Imams—are in Arabic. It is the combination of these factors that give Arabic the special status it enjoys among Muslims.

The Wretched State of the Jewry

Question

In the past, some Muslims were of the opinion that Jews will never have an independent country of their own. To support this view, they would cite some *hadiths* recorded in some Islamic sources. The establishment of the state of Israel, which has in the very short time since its inception become one of the most advanced Asian countries, proves this opinion to be incorrect.

Thus, is it not plausible that the *hadiths* in question were fabricated under the direction of those whose policy was to keep the people of this part of the world in ignorance by encouraging hypocrisy and animosity?

Answer

The governments of Great Britain, France, and the United Sates have occupied Palestine. They have granted a portion of this country to the illegitimate state of Israel, aiding it in every possible way. They have prevented Muslim countries from forming a united front against this false state.

In any event, the notion that some Muslims derived such a view from some *hadith*s recorded in some Islamic sources is incorrect. This notion is publicized by imperialist regimes in line with their policies to weaken people's faith in Islam. First of all, the view Muslims hold in respect to the fate of the Jewry is not as stated above, and, second, their view is derived from the Qur'an, not some *hadith*s.

After recounting the crimes and treacheries committed by Jews and exhorting Muslims to remain united in preserving the doctrines and practices of Islam, and warning them against befriending and following non-Muslims, God, the Exalted, says:

> *"Abasement has been stamped upon them wherever they are confronted—except for a relief from God and a relief from the people—and they earned the wrath of God, and poverty was stamped upon them. That, because they would defy the signs of God and kill the prophets unjustly; that, because they would disobey and commit transgression."*[129]

The "relief" from God and the people is clarified by the following two verses:

> *"O you who have faith! Do not take the Jews and the Christians for friends: they are friends of each other. Any of you who takes them as friends is indeed one of them. Indeed God does not guide the wrongdoing lot."*[130]

> *"Today the faithless have despaired of your religion. So do*

---

[129] Surah Al 'Imran 3:112

[130] Surah al-Ma'idah 5:51.

not fear them, but fear Me..."[131]

As you can see, the Qur'an promises the advance of Islam and the defeat of the Jewry, on the condition that Muslims comply with Islamic law and maintain unity. The verses, however, warn that should Muslims establish friendly ties with opponents of Islam, God will reverse the tide against them: Muslims will lose their prominence and non-Muslims will prevail.

But in spite of what I have said regarding this particular issue, there is no question that there are unauthentic *hadiths* in the Islamic corpus. This is a fact on which all Muslim scholars are in agreement. There is no need to resort to such gratuitous issues to prove the point. It is an accepted historical fact that after the death of the Prophet, some hypocrites and Jews, who only pretended to have embraced Islam, forged many false *hadiths*.

It is for this reason that before accepting a *hadith*, scholars of Islamic sciences apply a number of technical criteria designed to distinguish false *hadiths* from authentic ones. It is interesting to note that the Prophet had actually foretold that this will happen as is recorded in numerous *hadiths*, one of which is the following:

"If there reaches you [after my death] a saying from me, appraise it with God's Book; that which agrees with it, you should accept, and that which disagrees with it, you should slam to the wall [i.e., discard

---

[131] Surah al-Ma'idah 5:3; these two verses express that as long as Muslims are true to each other, refrain from pursuing friendly ties with opponents of Islam, and observe Islamic law ("fear Me"), they will enjoy God's guidance and, consequently, prominence. Otherwise, they will fail and others will prevail, thus providing relief to the Jewry to resume their unjust and domineering ways. How true are the words of God! This is exactly what plagues Muslims today. (Let me add that what 'Allamah states here is not an anti-Semitic expression. By Jewry, he, as the Qur'an, intends the greater majority of them that unfortunately hold racist views concerning other people.) [trans.]

it as unauthentic]."[132]

---

[132] See Amin al-Islam Abu 'Ali al-Fadl ibn al-Hasan al-Tabrasi, Majma' al-Bayan fi Tafsir al-Qur'an, vol. 1, p. 13, Mu'assisah al-A'lami li al-Matbu'at: Beirut, 1995.

Chapter 5: Human Origin and End

Question

About twenty years ago in Tabriz, in a literary circle, one of my friends mentioned a few points concerning determinism, freedom, and how human conduct is evaluated. He said that human beings return to the life of this world many times—between 80 to 100 times. Of course, they return not in the form of vegetables or animals, as some believers in reincarnation hold; rather, they return as human beings, and their affairs in each life is determined by their conduct in the previous life. It is only this explanation, he insisted, that could account for the many hardships and difficulties that people experience in this world.

Adam, for instance, sinned and was expelled to the earth. He died but was subsequently returned to the earth to receive the treatment he had earned in his previous life. All people undergo such consecutive lives. In each life they are different. In one life, they may be scholars, in others laypeople; in some they may be rulers, in others ordinary citizens; in some they may be beautiful, in others ugly; and so on and so forth.

It is only after living many lives and passing many tests that they earn what they actually deserve. It is based on this truth, he contended, that the Qur'an asserts that on the Day of Judgment no one will object to the evaluation of his deeds. This friend argued that if this was not the case, it would be unjust that one should turn out to be the Prophet and another Shimr.[133]

Another point that my friend made was that Adam was not literally an individual human being as I and you. He was the universal human being, subsuming in his existence all individual human beings, similar to a cluster of grape, which encompasses many grapes. As the human beings collectively sinned they were ousted from Paradise. If Adam was merely one individual human being who had sinned, why then should other humans bear the burden of his sin? To support this claim he also cited the Qur'anic verse that states that humankind made a pledge to God, indicating that all human beings were present along with Adam.

Another issue raised by this friend, which relates to the first point, was that if each individual had only one life and then died for good, the majority of humans would not deserve entrance into Paradise nor damnation to Hell. They would rather have a middle position, since the good and bad deeds of most people are equal.

This contradicts the Qur'anic division of humanity into the people of Paradise and the people of Hell. The only explanation that could account for such division, according to this friend, is that afforded by reincarnation [*tanasukh*]. After experiencing life in this world over and over again, it is then that people attain to what they deserve, whether it be damnation to Hell or entry into Paradise.

---

[133] In the tragedy of Karbala, the officer of Yazid's army who beheaded the Prophet's grandson, al-Husayn. [trans.]

Please respond to these questions.

Answer

To answer the questions raised above duly, one would need to provide detailed explanations. This, however, is not possible for me at present, for a variety of reasons. Therefore, I will treat these questions in brief, in the hope that the questioner will find his answer.

The belief that the soul returns to this world after death in another life is referred to as reincarnation. The advocates of this belief are, for the main part, idol-worshipers. They are of the opinion that if an individual succeeds in purifying his soul of all worldly impurities, he will attain union with God and, consequently, divinity. If, however, he fails to reach this lofty goal, there are two possibilities.

If he was virtuous in his prior life, he will return to this world in another body to be rewarded in worldly pleasures. This process will repeat, and each time he will be compensated in accordance with his conduct in the prior life. This is if he was virtuous in the previous life. If, however, he was evil, he will return to this world to be punished for his wrongs; he may degenerate into a lower form of existence, even possibly turning into an inanimate object. But, regardless of the person's moral state, reincarnation will continue indefinitely. It is based on this belief that believers in reincarnation deny a Day of Judgment and claim that the world is eternal.

This friend of yours, however, limits the number of reincarnations to 100. He believes in the Day of Judgment and in Resurrection but does not accept the idea of an individual progenitor for humankind.

He disagrees with the main advocates of reincarnation in that he accepts the Islamic notion of receiving reward or punishment in the Hereafter. Thus, his explanation of reincarnation is that the human being in the course of multiple lives attains to the status that is appropriate to him, but his requital will be delivered on the Day of Judgment. His argument for supporting this belief is grounded on several points.

First, one life is insufficient grounds for determining an individual's character. As such, any divine evaluation based on a single life would be arbitrary. To accept such arbitrary evaluation is tantamount to acquiescing to the notion of determinism (that human beings have no choice as to the life they lead, and it is God who predetermines one as the Prophet and another as Shimr). And the logical conclusion of determinism is God's injustice. Thus, if we wish to avoid this conclusion, we have no choice, this friend argues, but to embrace the doctrine of reincarnation.

Second, we know by the testimony of the Qur'an that on the Day of Judgment all creatures will accept God's evaluation of their conduct. This acceptance is undoubtedly due to their genuine agreement not out of fear of God's wrath, for that would implicate God's injustice. This friend claims that the only reasonable explanation for this agreement is the doctrine of reincarnation: those who receive a negative evaluation know that they deserve it, for they were given multiple chances, but they still failed.

Third, a single life is too short to offer all people equal opportunities. On the Day of Judgment, the thief could argue that he was penniless and so was forced to steal. One guilty of fornication could legitimately claim that the circumstances were not right for marriage, and so fornication was out of necessity. Hence, one life is too limited a basis for dividing humankind into the righteous, who go to heaven, and the evil, who end up in Hell.

These are the central points in your friend's line of reasoning. He is, however, incorrect on every account. First, his limiting the number of reincarnations to 80 or 100 is unwarranted. But in spite of that, the Qur'an—which treats of human life and conduct and eschatology in numerous verses—makes no mention of reincarnation. On the contrary, it states that there is only one life in this world:

"You were lifeless and He gave you life, then He will make you die, and then He shall bring you to life, and then you will be brought back to Him."[134]

"They will say, 'Our Lord! Twice did You make us die, and twice did You give us life. We admit our sins. Is there any way out [of this plight]?"[135]

The latter verse quotes those sentenced to Hell and unambiguously points out that humankind experience two deaths: one to the life of this world and another to the life of the Intermediate World [barzakh].

The first objection that this friend states is the problem of determinism. But if determinism is to pose a problem, a multiplicity of lives would not solve it. Suppose a person is reincarnated 100 times, and each time he commits a sin—say, murder. In such a case, the determinist will still hold that the punishment that the individual in question will receive on account of the murder is unjust, as he committed it involuntarily.

If, however, we side with the proponents of freewill, to which we are naturally inclined, we will acknowledge that when a sane adult commits a crime, he deserves due punishment. It is unreasonable to claim that one must commit a misdeed 100 times, for instance, in order to deserve retribution. In this light, Shimr's heinous decision to slay

---

[134] Surah al-Baqarah 2:28; according to this verse, the human being is brought to life, then he passes into the Intermediate World [barzakh], then he is resurrected on the Day of Judgment, and finally he attains to the final abode. Thus there is only one life in this world. [trans.]

[135] Surah al-Ghafir (or Mu'min) 40:11.

the grandson of the Prophet was his choice, and thus he alone bears the burden. God does not dictate anyone's life.

This friend's next premise is that people will willingly submit to God's judgment. From this, he infers that the human being experiences more than one life in this world, for otherwise he would be displeased with God's judgment. This inference, however, is awed. Humankind's submission to God's judgment is on account of their awareness that they had many opportunities in their worldly life to rectify their conduct, but they failed to take advantage of them.

The shame of their guilt will force them into silence. (In this relation, it is helpful to consider that all of what we have in this life, even our very existence, are God's bounties, which He has bestowed on us. Our relation to Him is one of absolute indebtedness, and this makes the burden of our guilt on the Day of Judgment even more onerous.)

This friend further contends that distinguishing righteous people from evil people is fortuitous unless they live more than one life. Again, this contention is invalid. Sound reason rules that three factors suffice in designating an individual as guilty or innocent: adulthood, sanity, and voluntary performance. When these three factors are present in an individual and he commits a misdeed, he is guilty, regardless of any other factor. This is the basis of law in all civilized societies, and it is also endorsed by Islamic law.

According to the Qur'an, we deserve the reward or punishment of every single deed we perform. For this reason, it exhorts believers to repent even if only for a single sin; one need not be an inveterate sinner to repent. Islamic law defines penalties—including the death penalty—even for individuals guilty of a single crime.[136] This is God's judgment in this world, and it is unreasonable to assume that it will be different in the Hereafter.

The above explanation makes clear that for most people one life is sufficient to determine their fate in the Hereafter. But in cases where a person's good and bad deeds are truly balanced, such that neither side prevails, those entrusted by God with the authority to intercede will secure his entrance to Heaven.[137] (Of course, this intervention is not arbitrary. It is granted to those who have faith in their worldly life but who commit too many sins to be allowed into Heaven on account of their conduct.)

Let us now consider more thoroughly Qur'an's treatment of this subject. In respect to the final outcome, the Qur'an distinguishes two groups: those who will attain to felicity in Heaven and those damned to Hell—

"As for the wretched, they shall be in the Fire... As for the felicitous, they will be in Paradise."[138]

This is in relation to the final outcome. At the time of reckoning, however, there will be three groups: the righteous who have earned

---

[136] Please note that 'Allamah's intention here is only to prove that we are responsible for every action we perform. Otherwise, Islam's penal code is very civil. For the execution of any penalty, there are a number of provisions that must be fulfilled. An extensive treatment of Islam's penal code is way beyond the scope of this book. [trans.]

[137] The following verse is one instance where the Qur'an mentions the doctrine of intervention:**"He knows that which is before them and that which is behind them, and they do not intercede except for someone He approves of..."** (Surah al-Anbiya' 21:28)

[138] Surah Hud 11:106-108.

their entry into Heaven, the damned who will certainly enter Hell, and the oppressed [*mustad'afin*], those whose cases are unsettled. Regarding the latter group, the Qur'an states:

> *"[They] are waiting God's edict: either He shall punish them, or turn to them clemently..."*[139]

And in yet another division, the Qur'an points to two groups of felicitous people:

> *"You will be three groups: the People of the Right Hand—and what are the People of the Right Hand? And the People of the Left Hand—and what are the People of the Left Hand? And the Foremost Ones are the Foremost ones."*[140]

This friend's other thesis is that Adam is the universal human being, not a particular individual. He supports this thesis with two lines of reasoning. First, the story of Adam's fall indicates that all human beings were present at the time. If Adam as a specific human being was exclusively to blame for the sin, it would be unjust for others to bear the consequence. We are still suffering from the consequence, and therefore, we are all guilty of that sin. Conclusion: we were all present at and complicit in that incident.

Second, the Qur'an states that prior to our existence in this world, God made us acknowledge that He was our Lord, lest we should claim on the Day of Judgment that we were ignorant.[141] This reveals that

---

[139] Surah al-Tawbah (or Bara'ah) 9:106.

[140] Surah al-Waqi'ah 56:7-11.

[141] See Surah al-A'raf 7:172-3. [trans.]

all human beings were created before this world and so were present when the primordial sin was committed.

His line of reasoning, however, is fallacious. We derive the story of Adam from the Qur'an, not from the Torah or the Evangel or any other mythic source. The Qur'an very clearly describes Adam as a human individual and the progenitor of humankind:

> *"O humankind! Be wary of your Lord who created you from a single soul, and created its mate from it, and, from the two of them, scattered numerous men and women..."*[142]

This verse declares Adam and Eve as the progenitors of humankind.

The other aspect of this thesis is to some degree true. That is, all human beings have the potential to attain to the status of Divine vicegerency, and so Adam was, as it were, humankind's representative: we are possessed of the same qualities that gave Adam his distinctive position. This is no indication, however, that human beings were actually present there.

But as regards Adam's sin, the popular conception is incorrect. The Qur'an makes it clear that prior to Adam and Eve's descent to earth, religion had not yet been ordained:

> *"We said, 'Descend together. When guidance comes to you from Me...'"*[143]

As such, it is incorrect to speak of sin, for sin is a violation of religious law. In this light, the prohibition on eating from the forbidden tree was not binding; it was an advisory warning, which God made out of

---

[142] Surah al-Nisa' 4:1.

[143] Surah al-Baqarah 2:38.

His love for Adam.

This friend argues that all human beings were present with Adam and abetted him in the primordial sin. The reason is that they are also bearing the burden: expulsion from Paradise and banishment to earth;

God would definitely not commit such an injustice as punishing the innocent. But this line of reasoning is, once again, false.

The truth is that God meant for humankind to live and procreate on the earth from the very start. When God intended to create Adam, he thus addressed the angels:

"...Indeed I am going to set a vicegerent on the earth..."[144]

The angels also knew that the human being was meant to live on the earth. This is evident from the following verse:

"...Will You set in [the earth] one who will cause corruption in it, and shed blood..."[145]

Even Satan knew that Adam and Eve's presence in Paradise was not permanent and that they had to leave in order to procreate:

"Said [Satan], 'Do You see this one whom You have honored above me? If You respite me until the Day of Resurrection, I will surely destroy his progeny, all except a few."[146]

aspect: procreative their to pertained them deceiving for contrived he stratagem the Thus,

---

[144] Surah al-Baqarah 2:30.

[145] Surah al-Baqarah 2:30.

[146] Surah Isra' (or Bani Isra'il) 17:62.

"Then Satan tempted them to expose to them what was hidden from them of their nakedness [i.e., their genitalia]..."[147]

Thus, the human being's presence in Paradise was a preparation for his descent to the earth, for ordainment of religion, and for his acquaintance with religious discipline. The degree of perfection that the human being can achieve in the earth with guidance from divine religion is much higher than what he had in Paradise before coming to the earth. Though life in the earth is aficted with hardship (the Qur'an says,

"..do not let [Satan] expel you two [Adam and Even] from Paradise, or you will be miserable..."1[148]

Also, He said:

"Certainly We created man in travail."[149]

But it is the prelude to the eternal life of the Hereafter. Life in this world is a test:

---

[147] Surah al-A'raf 7:20; in the Islamic tradition, the Forbidden Tree is not a source of knowledge of good and evil as the Judeo-Christian tradition has it (Genesis 2 and 3) but a source of sensual debauchery. Thus the Qur'an states that when Adam and Even ate from its fruit, they saw one another's private parts, of which they had previously been unaware. [trans.]

[148] Surah Ta Ha 20:117.

[149] Surah al-Balad 90:4.

"...We will inict on you good and ill as a test..."[150]

Through this test, the human being can achieve such a level of perfection as would be impossible without it.

---

[150] Surah al-Anbiya' 21:35.

Chapter 6: Divine Knowledge Possessed By the Prophet and the Imams

Imam Al-Husain's Foreknowledge that he would be Killed

Question

When Imam al-Husayn left Medina on his last and fateful journey, did he know that it would end in his martyrdom? In other words, did he set out on this journey with the intention to be killed or with the intention to establish a just Islamic state?

Answer

According to Shi'ah doctrine, the Master of Martyrs, Imam al-Husayn, was the third Imam and the Prophet's successor to Universal Authority [al-wilayah al-kulliyyah]. It is an article of Shi'ah faith—supported by doctrinal and rational reasoning—that the Imam possesses divine knowledge, which God reveals to him. Below I will examine how this knowledge affects the Imam's actions, especially with respect to Imam al-Husayn.

The Imam possesses knowledge of all that takes place in the world. This knowledge is granted by God to the Imam as His vicegerent. This knowledge transcends time and the sensible: the Imam knows the supersensible as well as the sensible, past and future as well as present. Numerous *hadiths* in the Shi'ah corpus support this doctrine, and so from a doctrinal point of view, it is indubitable.

One may object that a number of Qur'anic verses affirm that knowledge of the Unseen is exclusively God's. But the Qur'an also furnishes the answer to this question:

> **'[God] is the Knower of the Unseen; He does not disclose His Unseen to anyone, except to an apostle He approves of...'**[151]

This verse indicates that the other verses in question mean that God has this knowledge by His Essence and without the mediation of any other agent, whereas the Prophet, the Imams, and whoever else may possess this knowledge do so by God's command.[152] God bestowed it to the Prophet and thereafter to his rightful successors, the Imams.

There are a number of *hadiths* to the effect that the Prophet conveyed this knowledge to Imam 'Ali, and Imam 'Ali in turn conveyed it to his successors. But this is a truth that rational reasoning also corroborates. The Imam, as the most perfect creature, is the highest manifestation

---

[151] Surah al-Jinn 72:26-27.

[152] It is important to note that this pertains to all aspects of existence, not just knowledge of the Unseen. God is the only Self-sufficient and Necessary Existent. As such, all other beings depend on Him for everything, and so even our sensory perception depends on Him. [trans.]

of all Divine Names and Attributes.

This means that, like God, he possesses an all-inclusive knowledge. By his elemental essence [*al- wujud al-'unsuri*], he can know whatever he wishes. (This complex doctrinal question is obviously beyond the scope of this book. I have provided a thorough elucidation of it elsewhere.)

Based on what was said above, the Imam's knowledge is perfect; it is not affected by error. The source of this knowledge is the Secure Tablet[153], in which God's definite will as to the destiny of all things is recorded. Thus, the *Imam* knows all things as they are willed by God, and so he cannot in any way manipulate events using this knowledge.

As such, this knowledge transcends the domain of religious obligation.[154](Obligation is relevant only when one has a choice as to perform or not to perform a certain action. When, however, one knows that a certain event is inevitable, there is nothing he can do about it: the event will take place as determined by God's existential will.[155])[156]

The Imam knows the Divine decree but acts as his apparent du-

---

[153] "Secure Tablet": An allusion to Qur'an 85:22. [trans.]

[154] Religious precepts address the human being in so far as he is capable of fulfilling what it requires of him. It is unreasonable that a precept should obligate a task that the human being is incapable of executing. Now, with knowledge of the Unseen, the Imam knows what is going to happen, for instance, but he can do nothing to change it, for that is what God has willed. This is what 'Allamah means when he says that this knowledge transcends the domain of religious obligation. [trans.]

[155] This does not imply determinism. To say that an event has been decided by God is not to submit to determinism. God's will is such that it also encompasses human being's free will. That is, God knows eternally what every individual will do of his own accord. Thus, human volition also figures in.

[156] Existential will contrasts with God's legislative will. The latter designates the precepts He ordains; the former designates His will as the Creator and Lord of the world. When God wills something existentially, it will happen. But when He wills something legislatively, it means that He commands the human being to comply voluntarily; the human being may comply or disobey. [trans.]

ties—in so far as they are determined by apparent and external factors—require, while he is pleased at heart with what God's will has in store for him. This is evident in the last words Imam al-Husayn uttered before he was slain; lying in his own blood, he said, "I am pleased with Your decree, obedient to Your command. There is no one worthy of worship but You."[157] Also, in the sermon he delivered before leaving Mecca, he declared "We, the *Ahl al- Bayt*, are pleased with what pleases God."[158]

Imam al-Husayn acted in accordance with what the circumstances required, but this does not mean that he was unaware of his fate.[159] One may ask why Imam al-Husayn sent Muslim ibn 'Aqil to Kufah in spite of his knowledge that Muslim would be slain? Why did he leave Mecca? If in fact he knew that his fate was death, he should not have embarked on that journey, for the Qur'an says,

> *"..do not cast yourselves with your own hands into destruction..."*[160]

But the answer to all these questions is clear once the above explanation is understood.

The Qur'an states that the Prophet (and so by extension the Imams) led their life in this world, for the most part, as others do. They, as all other human beings, are possessed of freewill and perform their actions, normally; based on the knowledge they obtain through

---

[157] Ma'ali al-Sibtayn, vol. 2, p. 21.

[158] Ibn Tawus, Maqtal al-Husayn, p. 38, Beirut: Mu'assisah al-A'lami li al-Matbu'at, 1993.

[159] In fact, on a number of occasions, Imam al-Husayn alluded that his end and the end of those who remain faithful to him was martyrdom. See Ibn Tawus, Maqtal al-Husayn. [trans.]

[160] Surah al-Baqarah 2:195.

common means.

Thus, the Imam, like any other individual, assesses the harm and benefit in a course of action based on normal human knowledge, and once he is decided, he acts. If the circumstances are right, the Imam will succeed, and if not, he will, at least apparently, fail. This is because he is also bound by religious obligation. And as the leader, both spiritually and politically, of the Islamic nation, he is duty-bound to strive to spread the truth and uphold the cause of Islam.

A Historical Background on Imam Al-Husayn's Uprising

One of the darkest and harshest periods for the *Ahl al-Bayt* and the Shi'ah was Mu'awiyah's reign, which spanned two decades. After securing his absolute rule over the entire Islamic empire through deceitful stratagems, he turned his attention to consolidating his power and destroying the prominent status of the *Ahl al-Bayt* among Muslims. His intention, however, was not merely to destroy their prominence. He wished to erase their name completely. For achieving his purpose, Mu'awiyah was willing to utilize every possible measure—bribery, intimidation, torture, etc.

To this end, he persuaded a number of the respected companions (by various ways) to forge *hadith*s that praised the companions but damaged the status of the *Ahl al-Bayt*. By his command, the Master of the Faithful was dishonored from every pulpit, as if it were a religious rite. Mu'awiyah's agents—chief among them, Ziyad ibn Abih, Samarah ibn Jundab, Busr ibn Artat—were constantly on the lookout for *Ahl al-Bayt* sympathizers: when identified they were frequently killed.

These measures implanted in Muslims an aversion toward 'Ali and the *Ahl al-Bayt*, and the true believers who cherished the love of the

Ahl al-Bayt were forced to conceal their feelings. (The gravity of the situation can be grasped by noting that in the ten years of al-Husayn's imamate—which to the exclusion of the last several months coincided with Mu'awiyah's rule—not a single *hadith* was narrated from him.[161])

Despite this repressive atmosphere, however, Imam al-Husayn avoided open conflict with Mu'awiyah. For understanding why he chose to remain silent during Mu'awiyah's reign, one need only to consider the following reasons. First, Mu'awiyah had made al-Husayn pledge to refrain from challenging his rule. With this pledge in effect, he would have lacked public support to challenge Mu'awiyah.

Second, Mu'awiyah had established a respectable reputation for himself as a companion of the Prophet and a confident of the three caliphs prior to 'Ali; so much so that he secured for himself the honorific title

"Uncle of the Faithful" [*khal al-mu'minin*]. Third, considering Mu'awiyah's exceptional talent at deceit, it would have been very likely, if Imam al-Husayn had risen in open conflict, that he would contrive a plot to murder Imam al-Husayn through his agents then feign sympathy with the *Ahl al-Bayt* by killing the murderers.[162] (After all, it was Mu'awiyah who enticed Imam al-Hasan's wife into poisoning

---

[161] There are hadiths narrated from him by the subsequent Imams but not by Muslims from without the Ahl al-Bayt. This historical fact demonstrates how isolated the Ahl al-Bayt were.

[162] I think the reason why 'Allamah claims that this scenario would have been likely is that Mu'awiyah had executed a similar plot in the death of 'Uthman, the third caliph. Sensing the rising tension around him, 'Uthman asked Mu'awiyah for help. In a delayed reply to 'Uthman's request, Mu'awiyah sent an army toward Medina, the seat of caliphate, but ordered the general in charge of the army to set up camp in a certain location and wait for further orders. Despite 'Uthman's desperate entreaties, Mu'awiyah procrastinated until 'Uthman's death was announced. After getting news of 'Uthman's death, he called his army back and pledged to avenge 'Uthman's death. [trans.]

her husband.) It was for these reasons that Imam al-Husayn abstained from action during Muʿawiyah's reign.

Muʿawiyah's last blow to Islam was transforming caliphate rule into hereditary monarchy. He announced his son, Yazid, as the successor to the throne. But unlike his father, Yazid had no interest in even feigning a pious appearance. Yazid openly engaged in revelry: he brought musicians and dancers to his court, served wine, and made playing with monkeys a court game.[163]

Yazid knew that if Imam al-Husayn pledged allegiance to him, it would be the end of the *Ahl al-Bayt*'s prominence. So he was intent on obtaining Imam al-Husayn's allegiance, no matter what it took. Imam al-Husayn, on the other hand, was aware of Yazid's intentions. As the true leader and guide of the community of Muslims, Imam al-Husayn had to resist pledging allegiance to Yazid, for that would have been a fatal blow to Islam. But this resistance would cost al-Husayn his life, for Yazid wished one of two things. Preferably he wanted al-Husayn to acquiesce. If, however, al-Husayn resisted, Yazid wanted him dead and out of the way.

Imam al-Husayn was aware that resistance would lead to his death. But the interests of Islam required that he defy Yazid's authority. And this was the course on which he decided. He had no fears and was

---

[163] Of course, all this pointed to Yazid's lack of faith in Islam, which he shamelessly expressed after the incident of Karbala. As the prisoners of Karbala and the heads of the martyrs were being led into the city, Yazid reputedly heard a crow croak. As if inspired by the crow, he uttered this line of verse: "The crow croaked so I said, whether you are willing to say it or not, I settled my scores with the Prophet." And hours later when the prisoners were brought to his court, he sang the following line: "Hashim only played with power; otherwise there was no message [from the Unseen] and no revelation was revealed." [Hashim is the Prophet's great grandfather, after whom the Hashimite clan of Quraysh is named. The Hashimite clan of Quraysh, to which the Prophet belonged, and the Umayyad clan, to which Muʿawiyah and Yazid belonged, were enemies of old. [trans.]

determined to fulfill his obligation.[164] Ensuing events vindicated Imam al-Husayn's decision.

The brutal and ruthless way in which Imam al-Husayn and his companions were killed proved their innocence and rightfulness. Twelve years of political unrest followed, causing bloodshed and shaking the foundations of the oppressive regime. It was in this way that Muslims came to know the *Ahl al-Bayt*.

When relative calm returned during the imamate of Imam al-Baqir and Imam al-Sadiq, Muslims, in general, and the Shi'ahs, in particular, ocked to Medina to quench their souls from the fountainhead of light and truth—the *Ahl al-Bayt*. By sacrificing himself, Imam al-Husayn nourished the hearts of the faithful of all time with the love of the *Ahl al-Bayt*, a love that has been consuming an ever-increasing number of hearts over the past 14 centuries.

(Interestingly, Mu'awiyah had foreseen this end. On his deathbed, Mu'awiyah advised Yazid to refrain from taking action against al-Husayn if he refrained from pledging allegiance to Yazid. Mu'awiyah's advice to Yazid was not out of sympathy for the *Ahl al-Bayt*; rather, he knew that by killing al-Husayn, Yazid would immortalize him as a martyr and strengthen the status of the *Ahl al-Bayt*, and that would undermine the Umayyad rule.)

Thus we can conclude that Imam al-Husayn started his movement knowing that it would end in his martyrdom. He had realized that it

---

[164] A hadith reports that Imam al-Husayn saw the Prophet in a dream. The Prophet told him, "God wishes to see you slain." Another hadith reports that when some sympathizers tried to dissuade the Imam from challenging Yazid, the Imam said, "God wishes to see me slain." These hadiths should be construed in line with what was said above concerning the Imam's knowledge of the Unseen. Hence, "God wishes" in these hadiths refers not to God's existential will but to His legislative will. That is, the reason why the Master of Martyrs chose the path of martyrdom was that it was his duty and he wanted to fulfill his duty, not that he wanted to be killed because death was inevitable.

was his duty to stand up against Yazid's corruption and tyranny, though at the expense of his life. His duty was to awake the Muslim community from its slumber, and for this end, he chose the most effective method.

It is, however, important to note that all through his journey, Imam al-Husayn acted with wisdom, not rashness. He would take such steps as the circumstances required, and it was for this reason that he changed tactics in the various stages of his movement.

When the governor of Medina notified him that Yazid expected him to vow allegiance, he ed to Medina under cover of darkness. He took refuge in Mecca, God's sanctuary, remaining there until the *hajj* season, when he received information that Yazid had ordered his spies to kill al-Husayn during the *hajj*. By that time, people from Kufah had written thousands of letters to him, urging him to move to Kufah.

Kufis vowed to remain faithful to him.

To assess Kufis' sincerity, Imam al-Husayn sent his cousin, Muslim ibn 'Aqil to Kufah. After testing the waters in Kufah, Muslim wrote to al-Husayn that the people of Kufah were ready to support him and that he should set out at once. It was with these preparations that Imam al-Husayn decided to leave Mecca for Kufah. (An additional reason was that al-Husayn wished to preserve the sanctity of the House of God, which had never been defiled by bloodshed.)

But en route to Kufah, news reached Imam al-Husayn that his cousin had been killed. Since the Kufis had betrayed him and, consequently, establishing a just rule was no longer possible, Imam al-Husayn realized that the only way left to revive Islamic values was by shedding his blood. With this determination, al-Husayn made it clear to those who had accompanied him that if they remained with him they would be killed. Thus, the Imam marched toward his blessed end, where he and his companions were to be slain and his family taken captive.

Chapter 7: Refuting Wahhabi Contentions

The Question of Invoking the Prophet and the Imams

Question

Rational reasoning, the Qur'an, and the Sunnah all condemn invoking the Prophet and the Imams, which is practiced by the Shi'ah, as a heretical practice that amounts to polytheism. The reasons why this practice is heretical follow.

First, based on rational reasoning, God alone is the Creator and thus all causality springs from Him; the Qur'an avers,

> *"...God is the Creator of all things..."*[165]

In this light, the only real cause in the world is God. What we assume

---

[165] Surah al-Ra'd 13:16.

to be a cause is merely a thing that God has willed to occur prior to something else: there is no causal relationship among phenomena. When, for instance, timber burns, it is not due to a causal relation between it and fire; rather, it is the way God has willed to manage the affairs of this world. In the same vein, the Prophet and the Imams are merely creatures with no particular function, and so to invoke them would constitute polytheism.

Second, God says in His Book:

"Your Lord has said, 'Call Me, and I will reply to you.' Indeed those who are disdainful of My worship will enter Hell in utter humility."[166]

According to this verse, "calling" [*du'a*] is an act of worship. As such, to call on a creature of God is tantamount to worshipping it and is, consequently, an instance of polytheism.

Third, we know that the Prophet fought the beliefs of idol-worshippers and Christians though they all accepted God as the Creator of the world. The Prophet opposed them as they sought help from angels and invoked the souls of prophets to fulfill their requests. In this respect, the Prophet confronted Christians as he confronted idol-worshippers; both groups held polytheistic beliefs.

Fourth, according to the following two verses, only God has knowledge of the Unseen:

"...No one in the heavens or the earth knows the Unseen except God..."[167]

---

[166] Surah al-Ghafir (or Mu'min) 40:60.

[167] Surah al-Naml 27:65.

"**With Him are the keys of the Unseen...**"[168]

As such, no creature, not even the Prophet and the Imams, is aware of the Unseen. Obviously, for those who have died to this world and reside in the Intermediate World [*barzakh*], this world is "unseen," and so they are unaware of what transpires here. Thus, invoking the Prophet and the Imams, as they are dead, is, in addition to being a form of polytheism, useless. This argument is further strengthened by considering this verse:

"**The day God will gather the prophets and say, 'What was the response to you?' They will say, 'We have no knowledge. Indeed You are Knower of all that is Unseen.'**"[169]

In fine, invoking the Prophet and the Imams after they have passed away by showing humility and bowing to and kissing their tombs is definitely a polytheistic practice. So how do the Shi'ahs vindicate their practice?

Answer

The questioner first argues that there are no causes in the world, whether dependent or independent. As such, he denies the principle of causality by reserving agency exclusively for God. In addition to being contradictory to intuitive reason, two problems confront this line of reasoning.

First, it deprives us of the grounds on which we prove God's existence

---

[168] Surah al-An'am 6:59.

[169] Surah al-Ma'idah 5:109.

as the Creator. We reason to God's existence from the phenomena of this world. If we deny causality among phenomena in this world, we will be unable to argue for the dependence of this world on Divine activity. It would be ridiculous to talk about God arranging this world when we cannot prove His existence.

Second, to deny the principle of causality, one must also deny that a conclusion could follow logically from its premises. This would undermine the foundations of knowledge, leading inevitably to skepticism in every field of science.

We, however, owing to the Divine guidance imbedded in human nature, consider the principle of causality a universal principle that permits of no exception. All phenomena, being preceded by nonexistence, acquire existence from a higher cause. This higher cause may in turn have a yet higher cause, but the chain must end at a necessary existent (according to rational arguments that prove the impossibility of infinite regress and circularity).

This Necessary Existent, we call God—Exalted is He. Thus, the world is composed of causes and effects, headed by the Unique Cause who is independent in His agency. The agency of intermediate causes derives from God and as such is in effect God's agency.

That a being is a medium for conveying existence to other creatures does not imply its independence. For a better understanding of this, consider the following example. When one writes, the action of writing can be attributed to the person writing, to his arm, which holds the pen, and to the pen. Ascribing the action of writing to all three agents is correct, but the one which is independent and on which the others depend is the person.

So although the action can be attributed to the arm and the pen, but they are only secondary agents, they are merely means. In the example of fire cited by the questioner, the truth is that God has created fire with the natural quality of burning, not that fire issues from one act of creation and burning from another. God created the quality of burning by the mediation of fire, not independent of it.[170]

> *Hence, to affirm agency for God's creatures is not a challenge to His agency, for His is independent, whereas theirs is dependent. In fact, the Qur'an in ascribing various actions to creatures reaffirms the principle of causality but at the same time makes clear that independence in agency is solely God's. There are many verses to this effect; two examples follow:*
>
> **"Make war on them so that God may punish them by your hands..."**[171]
>
> **"...God only desires to punish them by means of [their wealth and children]..."**[172]

The questioner's next contention is that "calling" is an act of worship and so to call upon the Prophet and the Imams for help is polytheism. But it should be pointed out, in light of the above explanation, that "calling" God's creatures is conceivable in one of two ways.

One way is invoking a creature with the intention that it is independent in agency, and the other is invoking it as a medium. Accordingly, the verse in question

> *("Your Lord has said, 'Call Me, and I will reply to you.' Indeed those who are disdainful of My worship will enter*

---

[170] Thus, fire is the causal medium through which divine agency causes things to burn. [trans.]

[171] Surah al-Tawbah (or Bara'ah) 9:14.

[172] Surah al-Tawbah (or Bara'ah) 9:55.

Hell in utter humility."[173])

prohibits "calling" His creatures with the intention that they are independent in agency. Thus, monotheism condones invoking God's creatures if it is borne in mind that they owe their existence and agency to Him.

Obviously, if the verse in question were to be understood in a strictly literal sense as prohibiting any form of seeking help from God's creatures, we would have serious problems before us. We routinely go to the baker and ask for bread; we go to the butcher for buying meat; a strictly literal reading of the above verse would render these chores polytheistic. But we know for a fact that such cases of asking others do not constitute polytheism.

Some Wahhabi advocates have attempted to counter by pointing out that there is a difference here. In the cases cited, the people called upon are alive, whereas the Prophet and the Imams are dead. But this reply, if correct, only serves to demonstrate that calling on the Prophet and the Imams is useless, not that it is polytheistic.

Furthermore, there are verses that explicitly talk of "means":

"O you who have faith! Be wary of God, and seek the means of recourse to Him, and struggle in His way so that you may be felicitous."[174]

In this verse, God encourages believers to have recourse to the "means" that lead to Him as a way to attain felicity. In the same vein, there is a *hadith* narrated from the Prophet in which he says that faith and prayer

---

[173] Surah al-Ghafir (or Mu'min) 40:60.

[174]

are his means.[175] This *hadith* introduces these two elements (faith as a mental state in the believer and prayer as an action that the believer performs) as means for achieving nearness to God. If we were to accept a very strict reading of the verse in question (40:60), the employment of these means would be polytheism, and polytheism, obviously, does not lead to God.

The questioner's third point is that idolatrous religions agree with Islam in that there is One, Unique God, whom is worthy of worship, and that their error is in seeking help from other beings. This account of idolatrous religion is incorrect. According to their religious texts, idolatrous religions (which have hundreds of millions of adherents in such countries as China, India, and Japan), in spite of acknowledging that there is only One Necessary Existent, consider the Necessary Existent beyond the grasp of human knowledge: we are unable to communicate with the Necessary Existent directly. Thus, we need to worship mediums (such as angels, jinns, or spiritually perfect human beings) who are able to fill this gap and to help us draw nearer to the Ultimate Existent.

Angels are the deities whom idol-worshippers most commonly associate with. Idolatrous religions portray angels as pure beings who are close to God and whom He has entrusted with the governance of the world. As such, they believe that angels have absolute authority in their domain—there is a god or goddess for the seas, the deserts, war, peace, beauty, earth, sky, etc.—and that God has relinquished all matters to them.

The following verses bring to light the error in the polytheistic conception:

> **"Had there been gods in [the heavens and the earth] other**

---

[175] What is the source?

than God, they [i.e., the heavens and the earth] would have surely fallen apart...[176]

"...neither is there any god besides Him, for then each god would take away what he created, and some of them would surely rise up against others..."[177]

The line of reasoning in the above verses is that if there were a multiplicity of gods, they would have disagreed in matters of governance, and this disagreement would have led to chaos and destruction. Obviously, the underlying premise in this line of reasoning is that chaos would ensue if the gods had independent authority. Thus, the verses do not apply if there is one, supreme, and independent God but a multiplicity of subordinate agents who are dependent and obedient to God, functioning merely as His intermediate agents and executing solely what He desires.

The above explanation should suffice to show that idol-worshippers—whether those who worship stars or those who worship "the gods" of various creatures and phenomena—do not in any way worship God. Their rites of worship and sacrifice pertain to their pantheon of gods.

The only connection their worship has with God is that it is performed in the hope that their gods would inuence God and that only in regard to mundane affairs, for they do not believe in the doctrine of Resurrection. (It is in this context that the verse,

"...Who is it that may intercede with Him except with His

---

[176] Surah al-Anbiya' 21:22.

[177] Surah al-Mu'minun 23:91.

permission..."[178]

should be understood. This verse speaks to intercession in its broad sense, which includes worldly matters, not the prevalent sense of intercession on the Day of Judgment, in which the infidels of Arabia did not believe.)

There were, however, instances during the Age of Ignorance prior to Islam where idol-worshippers did worship God. But they did so out of ignorance of the logical implications of their belief system. One such instance was the *hajj*, the ritual pilgrimage established by Abraham. This practice endured even after 'Amru ibn Yahya succeeded in establishing idolatry as the predominant religion in the Arabian Peninsula. But some aspects of it were distorted. Idols, for instance, were set in holy locations—Hibil was placed atop Ka'bah, Asaf on Mount Safa, and Na'ilah on Mount Marwah—where they were worshipped and honored with sacrifices.

(It should be noted that idol-worshipping is actually a vulgarization of polytheistic doctrine. By doctrine, idols are supposed to be symbols for the deities. Common idol-worshippers, however, worship the idols themselves, as opposed to the deities they are supposed to represent. It is in condemnation of this vulgarized polytheism that the Qur'an says,

"...Do you worship what you have yourselves carved?"[179])

Hence, contrary to what the questioner claims, idol-worshippers neither consider God as in charge of the affairs of the world nor worship Him. Polytheists attribute an authority to the lesser gods that is, first, independent and, second, restricted to this world. They

---

[178] Surah al-Baqarah 2:255.

[179] Surah al-Saffat 37:95.

envisage the lesser gods as architects to whom God has given absolute authority to construct their world as they will. As such, they perceive God as the prime creator, who created the world but then resigned, relinquishing all authority to the lesser gods.

The questioner's next point is that Christians and Jews are polytheists. This, however, is incorrect. Christians and Jews are unbelievers on account of rejecting Prophet Muhammad's ministry, not for polytheism. The following verse ascertains this:

"Those who disbelieve in God and His prophets and seek to separate God from His prophets, and say, 'We believe in some and disbelieve in some' and seek to take a way in between—it is they who are truly faithless."[180]

In addition to denying Muhammad's ministry, they were also guilty for their absolute obedience to their priests and for believing in a son for God:

"The Jews say, 'Ezra is the son of God,' and the Christians say, 'Christ is the son of God.' That is an opinion that they mouth, imitating the opinions of the faithless of former times. May God assail them, where do they stray? They have taken their scribes and their monks as lords besides God, and also Christ, Mary's son; though they were commanded to worship only the One God, there is no god except Him..."[181]

(As regards Zoroastrians, the Qur'an does not give a detailed account of their religion. Historical sources, however, show that Zoroastrianism was polytheistic. Like idol-worshippers, they worshipped angels, but

---

[180] Surah al-Nisa' 4:150-1.

[181] Surah al-Tawbah (or Bara'ah) 9:30-31.

unlike idol-worshippers they did not carve idols to represent them.)

The above explanation makes clear that invoking the Prophet and the Imams as intermediate and dependent agents is not polytheism. Polytheism is to worship in addition to God other beings as independent agents. As such, to revere an intermediate agent while acknowledging its absolute dependence on the One God does not constitute polytheism. We know that the intermediate agent is in and of itself impotent. When, for example, a wealthy person helps a poor person through an intermediate agent, it is the wealthy person who truly deserves the credit, not the agent.

The questioner's fourth argument is that knowledge of the Unseen is confined solely to God. To consider others possessed of this knowledge is blasphemy. As such, the belief that the Prophet and the Imams are aware of and can interfere in what happens in this world is invalid: they are dead and for the dead, this world is "unseen." An examination of the Qur'an, however, would disprove this line of argument:

> **"[God is the] Knower of the Unseen; He does not disclose His Unseen to anyone, except to an apostle He approves of..."**[182]

According to this verse, there are beings to whom God divulges His secrets. Thus, there is no error in believing that God bestowed knowledge of the Unseen to the Prophet and the Imams. An observation that corroborates this view is that the Qur'anic verses that appear to deny the Prophet's knowledge of the Unseen make an exception in the case of Revelation:

> **"Say, 'I am not an exception among the prophets, nor do I know what will be done with me or with you. I just follow**

---

[182] Surah al-Jinn 72:26-7.

whatever is revealed to me...'"[183]

In Surah Ibrahim, the Qur'an narrates the answer that some prophets gave when their people denied that they held any special status:

> *"The prophets said to them, 'Indeed we are just human beings like yourselves; but God favors whomever of His servants that He wishes...'"*[184]

But the verse that very explicitly affirms knowledge of the Unseen for God's prophets is the following, which quotes the words of Jesus addressing his people:

> *"...I will tell you what you have eaten and what you have stored in your houses. There is indeed a sign in that for you..."*[185]

There is another verse in which Jesus announces the coming of Prophet Muhammad:

> *"I am the prophet of God to you...to give the good news of a prophet who will come after me, whose name is Ahmad..."*[186]

---

[183] Surah al-Ahqaf 46:9; what this means is that the Prophet does possess knowledge of the Unseen, but he does so because God has revealed it to him. No creature is capable of knowing the Unseen (or of anything else for that matter) independently of God. [trans.]

[184] Surah Ibrahim 14:11.

[185] Surah Al 'Imran 3:49.

[186] Surah al-Saff 61:6.

In addition, in the religious corpus, there are numerous *hadiths* that foretell future events, which are referred to as "forebodings."

Based on the above explanation, we can conclude that where the Qur'an denies that prophets possess knowledge of the Unseen and extraordinary powers, it means that independently they are incapable of knowing the Unseen or performing miracles. They do, however, possess these capabilities by God's will. God reveals the Unseen to His prophets and they convey it to their successors. There are many *hadiths* that substantiate this account.

> *There is, however, one verse that on the surface seems to pose a problem:*
>
> **"The day God will gather the prophets and say, 'What was the response to you?' They will say, 'We have no knowledge. Indeed You are Knower of all that is Unseen.'"**[187]

The verse seems to affirm that the prophets do not possess knowledge of the Unseen. A more careful consideration, however, refutes this conception.

If the prophets really lack knowledge of the Unseen, they would be unaware of their people's deeds. To be truly aware of a deed requires knowledge of the intentions that led to the deed in question.

Accordingly, to lack such a knowledge is equivalent to lacking knowledge of the deeds. But this cannot be, for the Qur'an asserts that the prophets do possess knowledge of their people's deeds; God's prophets witness their people's conduct:

> **"I [Jesus] was a witness to them so long as I was among**

---

[187] Surah al-Ma'idah 5:109.

them."[188]

"...That He may take witnesses from among you..."[189]

"...And the prophets and the witnesses will be brought..."[190]

"...And the witnesses will say, 'It is these who lied against their Lord...'"[191]

This reection clarifies that verse 5:109, which may be misinterpreted as meaning that prophets lack knowledge of the Unseen, actually means that of their own, they lack this knowledge, but by God's will, they possess it. In other words, all creatures, including all holy individuals, are indebted for what they have to God: all things are bestowed by Him.

The questioner's other claim is that showing respect to the tomb of the Prophet and the Imams is polytheism. But this, again, is incorrect. Tombs of holy personages are symbols [sha'a'ir] that remind us of God. Thus, to honor them is in essence to honor what they symbolize, namely God. Referring to the Prophet, the Qur'an says:

"...those who believe in him, honor him, and help him, and follow the light that has been sent down with him, they are the felicitous."[192]

---

[188] Surah al-Ma'idah 5:117.

[189] Surah Al 'Imran 3:140.

[190] Surah al-Zumar 39:69.

[191] Surah Hud 11:18.

[192] Surah al-A'raf 7:157.

And more generally concerning all Divine symbols, it states:

> *"...whoever venerates the symbols of God—indeed that arises from the God wariness of hearts."*[193]

Another way to vindicate the Shi'ah practice of honoring tombs of holy personages is by recourse to the following argument. Undoubtedly, loving God is a product of faith. When one loves God, one loves all those things that are in some way associated with Him. It is for this reason that all Muslims honor the Qur'an and the Ka'bah. All Muslims concur that it is an act of faith to touch and kiss the Black Stone.

Can any Muslim contend that this is a polytheistic practice? Obviously, not. It is in this spirit that the Shi'ahs revere the Prophet and the Imams and show respect to their tombs.

In fine, let me conclude by saying that it is surprising that the Wahhabis, who claim to uphold pure monotheism and condemn the Shi'ahs for showing respect to God's holy slaves, espouse the doctrine of the Eight Eternal Beings. Wahhabi theologians consider the Positive Divine Attributes—life, power, knowledge, audition, vision, will, and speech—to be eternal and external to the Divine Essence. They hold that these attributes have not been brought into existence by God and do not make up God's Essence. How can they so shamefully condemn the Shi'ahs, who merely honor those whom God loves, while in effect recognizing eight deities?

---

[193] Surah al-Hajj 22:32.

Chapter 8: Essence and Existence

Skeptics: Opponents of Realism

Question

In the history of philosophy there have always been anti-realists who claim that all our perceptions are illusory. The more radical ones even doubt their own doubt, thereby rejecting any possibility of real knowledge. In the sphere of philosophy, they are referred to as skeptics. Would you please provide a brief but reasoned philosophic argument against their position?

Answer

Skeptics are of three persuasions. Some skeptics say that the only realities whose existence we may ascertain are ourselves and our thoughts; all else is an illusion. The more extreme skeptics go even further, claiming that the only reasonable position to hold regarding knowledge is solipsism: only *I* and *my* thoughts are definitely real. The most extreme, however, doubt even their own doubt. According to the latter, knowledge is impossible. The falsity of this position, however, is definitively demonstrated in epistemology.

We know without doubt and based on our God-given intuition that there is a reality independent of and external to us. Against the skeptics, we hold that there are many real objects, each one of which is distinct from all others and possesses properties peculiar to it.

Each external object can in the mind be described by two concepts: essence and existence. The absence of either of the two concepts means that the object in question is illusory. Assuming that John is a real human being, the concept of John in the mind can be the subject of two predicates: human being, as its essence, and existence, indicating its objective reality.

Both of these concepts are critical if we are to believe that John really exists. Nevertheless, the two concepts are fundamentally different. *Existence* is the negation of *nonexistence*, and as such the two cannot concur. The two contradictory concepts may, however, be alternatively predicated of a thing's essence (in our case, *human being* as John's essence).

Another issue in regard to the two concepts, essence and existence, is that they cannot both be exemplifiable by objective reality, for if they were, every object would be in effect two objects—which is absurd. For this reason, one of the two is truly objective (i.e., it has objective instances) while the other is applicable to external objects only through the mediation of the objective one.

In other words, one of the two concepts is a mere abstraction and as such is exemplifiable owing to its concomitance with the objective concept. So the question is: which of the two is objective? To answer this question, it suffices to notice that a thing possesses objective reality only when existence can be predicated of it; its essence in and of itself may or may not exist.

Thus, it is *existence* that is objective, not the essence of the object in question. Based on this argument, the correct philosophic position is that existence is the objective concept. As such, the other views—mainly, the opposite view that essence is objective and existences subjective—are false.

Another issue that merits mention here is the gradational [*tashkiki*] status of existence. But first let us point out that logicians identify two types of universals: 1) those that permit of various degrees [*mushakkik*], 2) those that are not such [*mutawati*]. The universals that are of the latter type are instantiated by objects that partake of that universal in question equally.

For instance, *human being*: all human beings are equally human beings, and if there are any differences between the various individuals of this class it is due to the extrinsic qualities (e.g., height, weight, age) that are not contained in the concept of *human being*. On the other hand, a gradational universal is that whose instances differ in their exemplification of the universal in question.

Such as light: there are brighter lights and there are less bright lights; they are all instances of light, but they differ in regard to intensity, although this difference itself arises from the essence of light not from any extrinsic quality. The majority of the sensory qualities are gradational: visual qualities such as light (as was mentioned), distance, dimension; auditory qualities, that is, the various sounds; olfactory qualities, that is, the various smells; gustatory qualities, that is, the various tastes; and finally the tangible qualities.

The difference that distinguishes the various instances of these qualities lies in their very essence, not in any extrinsic quality (one distance is shorter than another; one sound is louder than another; one smell is more pungent or more pleasant than another; one taste is more delectable than another; one object is softer or warmer than another).

Of course, on examination one will realize that there is a subtle point here. The intrinsic difference elaborated above does not arise from the mental concepts that constitute our thoughts, but rather from their exemplification that occurs in external objects.

For instance, the color black: the variations in blackness pertain to the existential instances of the concept, not to the concept itself. This demonstrates that *tashkik* (intrinsic gradation) actually pertains to existence, not to essence as such. In this light, we may affirm the truth of intrinsic gradational variation, although in existence not in essence.

Furthermore, those who deny the existence of intrinsic gradational variation based on the reasoning that a single entity cannot at once satisfy contradictory qualities are wrong in that they are confusing numeric singularity with generic singularity. Their reasoning is correct only in relation to numeric singularity, whereas in generic singularity the simultaneous application of contradictory qualities is possible.

From the foregoing discussion we can conclude that a *mushakkik* is an entity that allows of intrinsic variation so that the difference that distinguishes its instances derives from the very reality that unites them.

After having considered these preliminary points, we can now turn to the concept of existence. The concept of existence as such can be predicated of all objects. The reality of the concept of existence, its external instance, is the locus where objective reality and properties of things obtain.

The external reality of the concept of existence accommodates a variety of opposing qualities and states—necessity and contingence, cause and effect, unity and multiplicity, actuality and potentiality, etc.—and as such is a gradational entity [*mushakkik*] that subsumes a plurality of degrees that vary intrinsically in intensity. In this light, it becomes clear that those who hold the concept of existence to be ambiguous [*mushtarak lafzi*], reecting the multiplicity of the essences of which it is predicated, are wrong. For, an essence is in and of itself neutral in regard to *existence* and *nonexistence*:

According to the definitive judgment of reason, both *existence* and *nonexistence* are predicable of an essence. Now, if the concept of existence were ambiguous, incorporating the meaning of the essence to which it is attributed (as our opponents claim) then to predicate nonexistence of an essence should constitute a contradiction—an obviously unreasonable conclusion. Their mistake arises from confusion between the properties of mental concepts and external objects, on the one hand, and from conating the relation of essence with the reality of existence and the relation of essence with the mental concept of existence.

Another opposing view is that the concept of existence has two meanings: one pertains to the Necessary Existent and the other to contingent existents. This wrong position also stems from confusing the properties of concepts with those of external objects. The difference between the existence of the Necessary [*wajib*] Existent and that of contingent [*mumkin*] existents is not ideal but ontic.

There is another false view in this regard to the effect that external objects are fundamentally distinct realities. The problem with this view is that we meaningfully predicate existence of all objects while it is impossible to derive a single concept from multiple objects that have nothing in common.

Another topic pertinent to the discussion at hand is the relation of existence [*wujud*] to essence [*mahiyyah*]. As was explained above, we derive two concepts from every external object: one indicates its essence and the other its existence. Clearly only one of these two is directly exemplifiable while the other refers to reality through the mediation of the directly exemplifiable one. Considering that the ontic properties of an object relate to that aspect of it from which the concept of existence is derived, we can conclude that *existence* is the directly exemplifiable of the two concepts, the essence being a purely abstract concept.

Of course, this should not be construed to imply that a thing's essence is an illusion that lacks any reference to objective reality. Rather, in saying that essence is an abstract concept, we mean that it is not immediately exemplified by external objects: its applicability to external objects is by means of existence, for a thing's essence is its existential boundary that sets it apart from other objects.

Thus understood, the view that a thing's essence is real only in the sense that is has objective instances is invalid. According to this view, the concept that comes into the mind and which we assume to portray truly the objective essence is merely an illusion. This line of reasoning runs in opposition to cogent philosophic arguments that prove that a thing's essence that is reected in the mind is essentially identical with the ontic essence of the object in question. It is for this reason that we are able to form true propositions by placing the essences reected in the mind as subjects and then describing them.

In addition, if we concede that the essences reected in the mind are merely subjective impressions, the hypothetical propositions formulated in various sciences would be doomed; even worse, any science that posits universal propositions should, on the basis of this conception, be discarded as chimerical. The physician would be wrong to assert that every human being has a heart. One would be justified only in uttering propositions that are confined to the objects one has directly observed. This position, however, would mean that all sciences should be forsaken.

Another consequence of this conception is that such logical definitions as species, differentia, substantial, accidental, etc. that we predicate of essences would also lose credibility.[194] Those who thus reject the validity of essences hold that such concepts are merely images of external objects similar to a picture one draws of something. The picture does not in any way define the object in question; it only reminds us of it. The falsity of this position, however, is very clear. For, if we have no way to truly perceive the external object, how can we tell that a certain image depicts the external object in question. Thus, we can condemn this conception as a blatant form of skepticism.

---

[194] This is a very complicated philosophic discussion whose thorough examination exceeds the scope of this work. Here 'Allamah merely alludes to topic. Those interested may refer to The Elements of Islamic Metaphysics, Sayyid 'Ali Quli Qara'i's translation of 'Allamah's Bidayah al-Hikmah. [trans.]

Chapter 9: Miscellaneous Questions

The Question of Imprecation

Question

In *"Al-Tafsir al-Mizan"* you say that even in this age any believer who encounters the appropriate situation may perform imprecation [*mubahalah*]. Can just any believer undertake this grave task?

Answer

There are indications in the Qur'anic verse in which the issue of imprecation is mentioned (3:61) from which we may deduce that it is a general practice, not a one-time event that happened between the Prophet and the Christians of Najran. Moreover, there are *hadiths* narrated from the Imams that clearly indicate that all believers may perform imprecation when the circumstances call for it.

In a debate that Imam al-Baqir had with 'Abd Allah ibn 'Umayr

Laythi on the question of temporary marriage, the Imam invites his opponent, when neither succeeded in convincing the other, to engage in mutual imprecation. In another *hadith*, the Imam advises a Shi'ah, who had been engaged in theological debates with some Sunni scholars, to call his opponents to enter upon mutual imprecation. Thus we can conclude that imprecation is a general solution that God has established in support of the defenders of truth.

The Inviolability of the Qur'an

Question

What is your view on whether the Qur'an has been distorted or not? Considering the fact that a certain Shi'ah scholar has written a book, contending that the Qur'an has been distorted, there are two questions that I would like you to address. One, what can we say in response to the Sunnis who condemn us for such issues? Two, how can the *hadith*s recorded in that book—averring that the Qur'an has been distorted—be justified?

Answer

The *hadith*s regarding the distortion of the Qur'an are numerous, relayed through both the Sunni and Shi'ah chains of transmission. Some traditionists [*ahl al-hadith*] have accepted these *hadith*s. The problem with these *hadith*s, however, is that they are self-defeating: to accept them would lead to rejecting their validity. For, the authenticity of *hadith* presupposes that the Imams are valid Islamic authorities. That in turn depends on the authority of the Prophet's words (as we believe that the Prophet appointed the Imams as his successors).

The authority of the words of the Prophet derives from the Qur'an as the most fundamental proof of his ministry. Now, to compromise the authority of the Qur'an by questioning its authenticity based on the possibility of its being distorted (whether that means extraneous material has been added to it or that certain parts of it have been deleted) would undermine the authority of the Prophet, the Imams, and finally the *hadiths* narrated from them. Thus, such *hadiths* are self-defeating.

The Infallibility of the Prophet

Question

A certain contemporary scholar, drawing on the works of Saduq, has written a treatise on the "Prophet's mistakes" [*Sahw al-Nabi*]. What is your opinion concerning this question? Moreover, why are such unnecessary topics even published?

Answer

Obviously, the Prophet is the perfect example, both in his speech and conduct, for every Muslim. For the Prophet to commit a mistake, considering his position, would be a grave error as it would jeopardize his mission and undermine his credibility as the guide chosen by God. This in turn would deprive the Qur'an and the prophetic *hadiths* of their authority, for there would be no guarantee that he did not err in relaying the Qur'anic verses nor in his sayings.

The Logic of Istikharah

Question

Is there a legitimate source on which the practice of *istikharah* (whether by the Qur'an or by the *subhah* [i.e., *tasbih*]) is based? Doesn't this practice degrade the Qur'an to the level of a book of soothsaying? Or how is it conceivable that the beads of the *subhah* could determine one's fate? Furthermore, why do some believers resort to *istikharah* before consulting with others [*istisharah*]? Would you not consider the prevalence of this practice a defect of the popular religious culture?

Answer

Regarding the practice of *istikharah* there are a number of *hadiths* related from the Imams. There is no rational or religious reason for discounting such *hadiths*. Furthermore, the logic of *istikharah* is very clear. When we decide to take an action, the first step is to contemplate its pros and cons. If we reach a conclusion, we act accordingly. But if our thinking doesn't produce a satisfactory conclusion, we then turn to others for consultation.

If consultation succeeds, we take the appropriate action. But if even after consultation, we remain undecided, it is only then that we may resort to *istikharah*. Holding the Qur'an in our hands, we ask God to help us. We then open the Qur'an at random and focus on the first verse that catches our attention. The option that the content of the verse points to is the one we take up.

This practice is actually a form of reliance on God, which is an indication of faith. For, from the various alternatives that we have before us, we choose the one toward which we think God has directed us. This practice is in no way unorthodox, and it is in no way harmful to the religious spirit. (This also holds in regard to *istikharah* by *subhah*.)

Chapter 9: Miscellaneous Questions

The Scripture of Fatimah [Mushaf Fatimah]

Question

Regarding the putative Scripture of Fatimah some Shi'ahs have published material in Kuwait in which the author describes the book as being several times larger than the Qur'an and in fact on a par with it. This has angered many Muslims around the world. What is your view concerning this issue?

Answer

In the corpus of Shi'ah *hadith* there is mention of a book which comprises Fatimah's sayings recorded by the Master of the Faithful. But to believe that such a book exists is not an article of the Shi'ah faith. It has never been regarded by the Shi'ahs as one of the religious sources that might rival the Qur'an and the Sunnah. Neither an Imam nor a Shi'ah scholar has ever adduced it in support of a religious position.

According to the related *hadiths*, the book in question tells of the secrets of the world and foretells future events. As such, to accept the existence of such a book is an innocuous belief. But it should definitely be underscored that no one considers this book as a rival of the Qur'an.

The Impermissibility of Exaggerating the Status of the Imams

Question

According to Shi'ah jurists, exaggerating the status of the Imams is heresy and those who hold such beliefs are heretics and thus *najis* (canonically impure). But what exactly does this ruling mean? How do we determine what constitutes "exaggerating the status of the Imams"?

Answer

To perceive the Imams as anything but God's servants would constitute exaggeration of their status: to ascribe to them attributes that are exclusively God's (such as creation and the governance of or interference in the existential affairs of the cosmos *independently*). Such a belief is heretical regardless of any other factor.

The point however that deserves to be emphasized is that it is the *independence* factor that is problematic. That is, to attribute Divine qualities to a creature, believing that it possesses them independently is heretical. However, to consider a creature as possessed of *existential authority* and thus an intermediary of Divine effusion (as we all believe that the Angel Mika'il is entrusted with providing sustenance to creatures, the Angel Jibra'il with the conveyance of Revelation, and the Angel Izra'il with the task of extracting souls at death) is another issue that does not constitute exaggeration.

The Occurrence of "Li Allah-I Darr-U Fulan" And "Kana Li Allah-I Rida" In Words of the Commander of the Faithful

Question

In a few instances in the *"Nahj al-Balaghah"* we come across such contradictory phrases as *"li allah-i darr-u fulan"* ("It is upon God to reward Him")—which is complimentary—and *"li allah-i bala'-u fulan"* ("It is upon God to assail him with an afiction")—which is condemnatory—in reference to the *khulafa'*.

Further, in a letter to Mu'awiyah, Imam 'Ali refers to pledging allegiance to the *khulafa'* as *"kana li allah-i rida"* ("Therein was God's satisfaction") whereas in other instances, specifically in his Shaqshaqiyyah speech, he denounces the *khulafa'* as unrightful rulers. What are we to make of these contradictory statements?

Answer

First of all, it should be noted that the connotation of *"kana li allah-i rida"* ("Therein was God's satisfaction") is different from that of the other two statements you have mentioned.[195] The former can be interpreted in one of two ways. First, it is possible (since it is in a letter addressed to Mu'awiyah) to say that the Imam does not really mean it; rather, he is saying this in line with the prevalent view of the day.

Second, it is very likely that it means that although the Imam disagreed with what took place after the Prophet's death, but he conceded

---

[195] That is, the connotation is not such that it could be examined in a comparison with the other two statements. [trans.]

in order to preserve the unity of the *ummah*, for otherwise the very existence of the nascent Islamic state would have been compromised; it was this unity that God pleased although the usurpation of Imam 'Ali's authority was indubitably in violation of God's command.

But as for the other two statements—*"li allah-i darr-u fulan"* and *"li allah-i bala'-u fulan"*—they are clearly in reference to the *khulafa'* and the rulers appointed by them. As regards the second statement (i.e., "It is upon God to assail him with an afiction"), which is condemnatory, the meaning is evident. But as regards the first statement (i.e., "It is upon God to reward Him"), which is complimentary, it should be understood in light of Imam 'Ali's effort to maintain unity and peace in the Muslim *ummah* (for which purpose he abstained from voicing his opposition and discontent for 25 years), not as a frank statement of his view. For, according to the thousands of *hadiths* related from the Imams—one of which is Imam 'Ali's Shaqshaqiyyah speech—the true successor of the Prophet, designated by God, was 'Ali, but his position was usurped.

A Call to Unity and Brotherhood

Question

It is a historical fact that Imam 'Ali, in the interests of the Muslim *ummah*, pledged allegiance to the *khulafa'*. Considering this fact is it appropriate to curse those who ruled the Islamic state in its formative period? Is it not being more Catholic than the Pope to feed the sectarian tension? No doubt, we encourage serious scholarly discussions on questions of faith, but to maliciously provoke the religious emotions of our Muslim brothers is not religiously justifiable.

In fact we have seen the founding of the Center for the Union of the Islamic Confessions [*Dar al-Taqrib bayn al-Madhahib al-Islamiyyah*] in

Cairo, Egypt, which is supported by such eminent Shi'ah scholars as Ayatullah Burujerdi and Ayatullah Kashif al-Ghita'. It has produced significant results, such as Shaykh Mahmud Shaltut's [196]*fatwa*, recognizing the Shi'ah confession as one of the orthodox denominations of Islam.

Would it not be better to pursue this path, holding scholarly discussions between the highest authorities, rather than to condone the unchecked activities of radical groups, whether Shi'ah or Sunni, which are manipulated by our common foes?

Answer

Let me first make this point that unity in the sense of neglecting one's religious doctrines and erasing the confessional distinctions is unreasonable. Nevertheless, we must strive to achieve unity on the common grounds that exist. In the early history of Islam, Muslims succeeded in pervading a great part of the civilized world in less than a century after Islam's inception. But unfortunately that magnificent power gradually faded as the result of a lack of unity and forgetting the social aspect of Islam. Of course, the role of the enemies who relentlessly struggled to create strife between the two main branches of Islam should not be overlooked.

To regain that power, we should emphasize that the differences that separate the two confessions are in the minor practices; we all agree on the main doctrines of faith and the main practices: *salat* (canonical prayer), fast, *hajj*, *jihad*, etc.; we all pray facing the Ka'bah and read the same Qur'an.

It was in this spirit that the Shi'ahs of the early period of Islam remained alongside the majority Sunnis, contributing to the common

---

[196] Dean of the Al-Azhar Islamic University in Cairo.

interests of the Islamic state and giving advice and counsel where needed.

So too today it is incumbent on all Muslims to bear in mind their common beliefs, realize the oppression to which the imperialist powers have subjected them, and lay aside their sectarian quarrels, thus forming a united front against the common foes of Islam.

Fortunately Muslims are awaking. Thus, the idea of Islamic unity was put forth by the Shi'ah *maraji'*[197]. It was welcomed by a strong support from the honorable Shaykh of Al-Azhar, who introduced to the world the fundamental unity of the Shi'ah and Sunni. We, Shi'ahs, must be thankful of him for this great, and no doubt sincere, service.

As you [i.e., the questioner] have also pointed out, scholarly discussions between Sunni and Shi'ah scholars are in no way detrimental to this unity. Such discussions should persist so as to eradicate the darkness of ignorance and shed light on the truth, such that all would realize it—this is not dogmatism.

> *We beseech God that He guide the malevolent characters who strive to spread corruption and that He aid the Muslims in consorting their efforts so as to reclaim their past superiority.* **"Verily He is All-hearing, answering those who beseech Him."**

The Concentration of the Prophets in the Middle East

Question

Why are all the prophets from the Middle East region: Arabia, Egypt, and Shamat? Why there were not prophets in other regions of the

---

[197] Maraji': pl. of marja', in the Shi'ah, the equivalent of the Sunni mufti. [trans.]

world—say, in Europe or Australia?

Answer

There is no evidence that could prove that the prophets lived only in the Middle East region to the exclusion of other parts of the world. That the twenty-odd prophets mentioned in the Qur'an were in this region does not mean that other parts of the world did not have prophets. In fact, verse 24 of *Surah Fatir* affirms that all nations have had their prophet:

> *"...and there is not a nation but a warner has passed in it."*

Difference in Capabilities

Question

Creatures differ, from the very start of their existence, in their capabilities and capacities. For instance, one is blessed with the capacity to receive the grace of prophethood; another is granted the privilege of *wilayah*; this, while the majority of creatures lack such special blessings. What is the reason for these differences?

Answer

All creatures have some potential, which is realized in a variety of manifestations depending on the circumstances. Elemental matter has the potential of becoming vegetative; plants, in turn, have the potential to bear fruit; fruit possesses the potential to grow and become a full-grown plant; semen, after resting in the female reproductive organ of an animal, has the potential to grow and take the form of that particular animal. Now, as to the agent that affects these potentials, it is without question an immaterial being.

As to the question posed above regarding the difference in the potentials of various creatures, that question should be sought in connection with the topic of final causality. Thus, to state the question more accurately we must ask, what is the *purpose* for creatures' being endowed with different capabilities, thus receiving the Divine effusion in various degrees?

> *Why did not God create the world such that His Effusion would encompass all creatures equally, leaving no room for evil, corruption, and imperfection? The answer in a word is: the cosmic purpose of the universe is that the most perfect creature, the human being, should come into existence.*
>
> *"...It is He who created for you all that is in the earth..."*[198]
>
> *"And He has disposed for you whatever is in the heavens and whatever is in the earth..."*[199]

Human nature pursues perfection. In order to achieve perfection, he must undergo many trials and tribulations. This in turn requires that there be differing potentials in the world, for otherwise there would be no tribulations.

Some Questions Regarding the Story of Moses and Khidr

---

[198] Surah al-Baqarah 2:29.

[199] Surah al-Jathiyah 45:13.

Question

The story of Moses and Khidr related in the Qur'an raises several questions. One, how can Khidr's destruction of another's property—where he made a hole in the bottom of the boat they were traveling in—without permission be justified? Two, was his slaying of the young boy not an instance of prosecution before the commission of crime? Three, what was the treasure buried under the wall? Four, what made Khidr eligible to act as teacher to Moses, the bearer of prophethood of his time and the locus of Divine knowledge on earth? (The same question arises with regard to the story of Rubil the Shepherd's counsel to Jonah and the replies of the woodpecker and the ant to Solomon.[200])

Answer

Such incidents as death and destruction of property happen regularly in accordance with God's decree. These incidents are not crimes when considered in relation to God. For, He is the owner of the entire creation and the legislator and as such is not bound by what He legislates; what He does is certainly out of justice and for good. Khidr's statement,

> *"...I did not do that out of my own accord..."*[201]

clearly indicates that his actions, whose purpose he revealed to Moses, were executed in submission to God's existential decree, not His legislative decree, and thus were not subject to religious law.

---

[200] See Surah al-Naml 27:18 and 22.
[201] Surah al-Kahf 18:82.

Furthermore, although Moses was superior to Khidr, there was no wrong in him learning certain things from Khidr who was inferior to him.

The same case holds true with regard to Rubil the Shepherd's counsel to Jonah. As to the woodpecker's reply, it only suggests that the woodpecker had directly witnessed the court of Sheba whereas Solomon had not; there is nothing wrong in that. Finally, the ant's warning to the colony was only to save them from being trampled on by Solomon's army, and that the ant was blunt was of no harm.

Legislative Authority

Legislative Authority [Al-Wilayah Al-Tashri'iyyah]
Question
What is the legislative authority [al-wilayah al-tashri'iyyah] of the Prophet and the Imams you mention in *"Tafsir al-Mizan"* in commenting on verse 55 of *Surah al-Ma'idah*.

Answer

Legislative authority is the authority to govern human society and manage the affairs of the Muslim nation in accordance with Islamic law. In a word, it is the authority to head the Islamic state.

The Meaning of Indhar (Warning) in Reference To Animals

Question

> "...There is no animal on land, nor a bird that ies with its wings, but they are communities like yourselves..."[202]
>
> "And there is not a community but a warner has passed in it..."[203]

Considering the above two verses together, one may infer that animals also have warners and thus are duty-bound [*mukallaf*]. Is this inference valid?

Answer

Indhar is to warn people against God's punishment. As such, it is part and parcel of the heavenly religions ordained by God. However, an examination of the verses of the Qur'an proves that the verse quoted above pertains to human beings alone.

Adam's Deception by Satan

Question

> The following two verses seem to contradict the account of Satan deceiving Adam:

---

[202] Surah al-An'am 6:38.
[203] Surah Fatir 35:24.

*"Indeed as for My servants you do not have any authority over them."*²⁰⁴

*"Indeed God chose Adam and Noah, and the progeny of Abraham and the progeny of Imran above all the nations."*²⁰⁵

How can the content of these verses be reconciled with Adam's being deceived into eating from the fruit of the forbidden tree?

Answer

According to verse 38 of *Surah al-Baqarah*

("We said, 'Get down from it, all together! Yet, should any guidance come to you from Me, those who follow My guidance shall have no fear, nor shall they grieve.'"),

religion was established after the Fall. Also, the special status that God's special servants enjoy (in being immune from Satanic temptations) as described in verse 15:42 pertains to this world. Moreover, according to verse 122 of *Surah Ta Ha*

("Then his Lord chose him, and turned to him clemently, and guided him."),

Adam's promotion to the status of the special servants took place in this world. So, since religious law was established in this world and Adam was chosen as one of the special servants again in this world,

---

²⁰⁴ Surah al-Hijra' 15:42.
²⁰⁵ Surah Al 'Imran 3:33.

there is no inconsistency among the verses cited in the question, for Adam ate from the fruit of the forbidden tree prior to this world. Based on this line of reasoning, in eating from the fruit of the forbidden tree Adam did not disobey God; rather, he neglected God's advice.

A Question Regarding the Incident of The Moon Splitting In Half

A Question Regarding the Incident of The Moon Splitting In Half [*Shaqq Al-Qamar*]

Question

How can the story of the moon splitting in half at the request of the Prophet, recounted in both the Qur'an and the Sunnah, be rationally explained, especially considering the fantastic details related in some *hadiths*?

Answer

That such a miracle was performed by the Prophet is beyond doubt as it is attested by both the Qur'an and the Sunnah. As to the details, however, the *hadiths* disagree. Since the *hadiths* that recount the incident are not ascertainable when taken individually, the details provided therein are dubious. What can be said with certainty is that the Prophet pointed to the moon, which caused it to split in half. This much of the story is verified by the Qur'an—

"*The hour has drawn near and the moon is split.*"[206]

---

[206] Surah al-Qamar 54:1.

—and is thus indubitable. The Prophet executed this miracle in reply to those who rejected his ministry on the pretext that they needed to see him perform a miracle. As this miracle is confirmed by the Qur'an it is beyond doubt. This is as far as this story is concerned.

As to the general topic of miracle, it cannot be refuted by rational reasoning, though one may be reluctant to accept the possibility of such phenomena. Miracles are executed through the interference of higher agents—of which most of us are utterly ignorant—in the normal function of natural agents.

Some have claimed that the moon's splitting in half was not a miracle performed by the Prophet. They claim that the verse refers to an apocalyptic incident that will occur on the Day of Judgment when God will destroy the material world. This reading, however, is disproved by the context. The next verse (*Surah al-Qamar* 54:2) clearly indicates that the splitting of the moon referred to in the first verse is a miracle that actually took place during the life of the Prophet:

> *"If they see a sign, they turn away and say, 'An incessant magic!'"*

Clearly enough, if the splitting of the moon referred to in the first verse were to take place on the Day of Judgment, the unbelievers could not reject it as magic.

Still others contend that the verse in question refers to the scientifically confirmed phenomenon of the separation of the moon from the main body of Earth during the primitive stages of its development. They cite this as proof of Qur'an's veracity as it, in their view, told of this phenomenon many centuries before science. This contention, however, is refuted by a lexical consideration of the verse at issue. To signify the separation of one object from another—whether by way of reproduction or detachment—in the Arabic language, the words *ishtiqaq* and *infisal* are employed, not *inshiqaq*, which signifies specifically the splitting in half of a single object.

Another objection that has been made against the miracle account is that if such an extraordinary incident had occurred, non-Muslims would have also recorded it. This objection neglects the fact that those who record history do so in accordance with the interests of the powers who patronize them.

Any incident or event that is against the interests of the powers would go unrecorded and thus doomed to oblivion. It for this reason that we find no sign of the story of Abraham, Moses, or Jesus in the conventional annals of history, although from the religious point of view there is no doubt in their miracles and accomplishments: Abraham was catapulted at the behest of Nimrod in an enormous fire without being harmed; Moses exhibited his miraculous staff and white hand; Jesus brought the dead back to life. Furthermore, it should be noted that there is a considerable time difference between Mecca, where the miracle occurred, and the Western hemisphere. As such, one cannot expect that this extraordinary lunar event, which appeared for only a very brief time, should have been descried in such Western countries as Rome and Athens.

An Unfounded Myth

Question

Is the story of Venus alighting on the roof of the Master of the Faithful's house supported by authentic sources?

Answer

This story is related in a few *hadiths* that are neither *mutawatir*[207] nor ascertainable [*qat'i al-sudur*] and thus are unreliable.

A Question Regarding the Islamic Penalty of Severing the Hand of the Thief

Question

Why does Islam order the hand of the thief to be cut?

Answer

In examining the Islamic penalty for theft, which is to sever four fingers of the thief's hand, two aspects should be distinguished: first, that in committing a wrong the thief deserves to be punished and, second, that this punishment should be the severing of the hand. Considering the first aspect, we know that Islamic law is not alone in setting a penalty for theft.

Human societies, as far back as history sheds light on, have invariably condemned theft and punished thieves; this includes primitive human communities, tribal societies, feudal societies, monarchies, theocracies, and finally democracies. This universal consensus is based on the belief that the most valuable asset that human beings possess is life and that the foremost responsibility of the individual is to pursue a felicitous life.

---

[207] In the science of hadithology, this term refers to a hadith whose chains of transmission are so numerous that it is beyond doubt. [trans.]

To this end, people work collectively as a society to acquire wealth and secure their welfare. In this way, people expend one half of their life—an invaluable price—to secure the well-being of the other half.[208] As the importance of safekeeping a goods increases in proportion to its value, it should go without saying that to keep our possessions—for which we have expended one half of our life—safe is of utmost importance.

Thus, to leave the possessions of the individuals of a society unprotected is tantamount to destroying one half of the collective life of that society just as leaving the lives of the constituent individuals of a society unprotected is tantamount to destroying the entire collective life of that society:

> "...whoever kills a soul, without its being guilty of manslaughter or corruption on the earth, is as though he had killed all mankind..."[209]

In this light, thieves as enemies of the financial security of the society must be dealt a severe punishment that would also serve as a deterrent.

As to the second aspect of the question, that is, the punishment that Islam designates for this crime, one can infer on examining the entire body of the Islamic penal code that the rationale that Islam pursues in the punishments it establishes is to inict upon the criminal the like of which the victim has suffered so that, first, he would receive the justice he deserves and, second, it would make a lesson for other potential criminals.

Obviously, it is not possible to recompense for a wrong that ruins one

---

[208] That is, people spend a good part of their life working to procure the necessities and comforts needed to lead a happy life. [trans.]

[209] Surah al-Ma'idah 5:32.

half of an individual's productive life by monetary fine, whether small or large, or imprisonment. The strongest proof for this is the failure of such measures to achieve their purpose in the so-called advanced countries. Heeding this realistic analysis, Islam orders the hand of the thief, which is more or less equal to one half of his life's work, to be severed.

Unfortunately, the objections that our so-called enlightened thinkers make against Islam's penal code—which have these days become as ubiquitous and ruinous as theft in our country—shows that they do not realize this very clear logic. Their argument is, why should a man's hand—which God has bestowed to him for the pursuance of his wellbeing and which he has the right to utilize throughout his life for resolving his problems—be severed as the result of a mistake he committed under financial pressure?

What this argument does is in essence to justify the wrong perpetrated by the thief and then to evoke our sense of pity to feel sorry for him. The error in this line of reasoning is very clear. Although it is a virtue in personal issues to be clement and forgiving in treating those who have wronged us (as Islam strongly encourages the victim to relinquish his right to punish the offender), to be sentimental in dealing with social issues is wrong. To be lenient toward criminals is a ruthless injustice toward the society at large; in leaving the thief free and respecting his "human rights" we would be harassing and disrespecting the innocent individuals of the society. In the words of Rumi:

> "To pity the sharp-toothed leopard is to oppress the sheep."

So the issue is that in the legal code, the legislator must ensure the interests of the society at large, not merely the individual welfare of the thief or even the victim for that matter.

Let us now turn to another objection that is closely related to what has thus fur been elucidated. The objection is that there should be a difference between a thief who is driven to commit a petty theft out of need and desperation and one who has made this crime his vocation, continually offending the public, everyday ruining the happiness of a family.

Why, then, does Islam treat both cases similarly? The answer is, when Islam establishes a certain punishment for a crime, it is enforceable when the judicial authority of the Islamic state has confirmed the commission of the crime. If one commits theft once and is thereafter apprehended and proven guilty he receives the punishment of the severance of four fingers of the right hand; one will receive the same punishment if he is apprehended after having committed theft more than once without being punished.

Furthermore, the Islamic penal code treats all instances of theft, whether grand or petit, equally, for both cases are violations against one of the fundamental elements of the society—namely, financial security. The conditions and circumstances that lead up to the commission of theft make no difference in the execution of punishment.

The detractors of Islam's penal code further argue that by cutting the four fingers of the thief we render him a public burden as he can no longer care for himself, not to mention that one potentially productive member of the society is incapacitated.

These gentlemen should be reminded that in a country with a diverse population with multifarious needs, there will definitely be work for someone missing four fingers; he would not constitute a burden for the society. It is precisely for this reason that the next punishment Islam assigns for one who repeats the crime of theft is not the severance of the other hand but the severance of his left foot.

Moreover, assuming that the incapacitation of a thief does constitute a burden for the society, is this burden not incomparably lighter than the financial insecurity that his offense brings on the society? What a ridiculous argument! Is the incapacitation of a thief more burdensome on the society than leaving him unrestrained or than imposing on the society the heavy costs of keeping him imprisoned?

Are the ever-increasing number of thieves and burglars in our country not a public liability? They continue their evil work unrestricted, preying on the efforts of others. And this is not to mention the murders and other shameful crimes that they naturally inict on their victims in the process of theft, the accounts of which abound in our newspapers.

Thieves caught under the present law are crowded in prisons. Does imprisonment yield any benefits other than the leisure it affords the criminals at the expense of the society and the opportunity it provides for criminals to enhance their expertise in the company of their more experienced colleagues.

The detractors in turn make the point that such cruel punishments are incapable of advancing the deterrent function that is expected of them. This is clearly demonstrated, in their opinion, by the failure of the American movies depicting the life and fate of criminals in decreasing the crime rate; such movies have only helped to increase the crime rate.

But how could they expect such exciting and sexually provocative movies, which more often than not exonerate criminals and portray as libertinism the happy way of life, to help in reducing the crime rate? The example of such movies should in no way be compared with the punishments established by Islam. Sound judgment definitely rules in favor of such criminal punishments as measures that dissuade those who are tempted to violate the law. Of course, social factors, like natural factors, are not absolute. Thus the advocates of the Islamic penal code do not claim that such punishments would absolutely uproot crime; they would however reduce crime rate to a minimum.

Chapter 10: Some Qur'anic Questions

A Question Concerning the Separate Letters that Open a Number of the Surahs of the Qur'an

Question

We know that God revealed the Qur'an to the Prophet gradually and intermittently. The sum of its verses is 6216 according to Ibn Sirin and 6218 according to Ibn Mas'ud.[210] All are agreed, however, that there are 114 *surahs*. Twenty eight of these *surahs* begin with the *separate letters* [*al-huruf al-muqatta'ah*]—viz., *alif-lam-mim, alif-lam-ra', alif-lam-mim-sad, ha-mim, ta-sin, ta-sin-mim, ka-ha-ya-'ayn-sad, ya-sin, sad, ta-ha, qaf, nun*. Now, the question is: why do they open 3 Madani and 25 Makki *surahs*? Why don't they appear at the beginning of all *surahs*?

---

[210] The difference in numbering is solely a matter of pagination. In other words, the disagreement between Ibn Sirin and Ibn Mas'ud revolves around their respective opinions as to the intervals at which the numbers of the verses should be placed. Otherwise, they both agree on the exact content of the Qur'an. [trans.]

The Qur'an was revealed in Arabic; the Prophet's Companions received it from his mouth and preserved it, some by writing, some by heart; one would expect that they understood these letters. But if they had understood the meaning of these letters they would have not given such divergent views about them.

We know that these letters have meaning, but what is their meaning? Are they secret codes or acronyms or are they just intended as attention-grabbers?

I have for long been contemplating exegetic *hadith*s and the sayings of the Companions; I have mulled the explanations put forth by various exegetes and orientalists; I have considered the esoteric interpretations of the Sufis. None shed light on this enigma.

As the Qur'anologists disagrees on this question, I decided to ask for your view, hoping that it would clear my doubts and answer my questions. Please give me an answer that would shed light on this matter (in which case I would be greatly beholden to you) and do not tell me they are Divine secrets known only to God: the Qur'an was revealed in Arabic, a human language, for the guidance of humankind.[211]

Answer

I offer my most sincere greetings to you and apologize for the delay. When your letter reached Qum I was in Damavand, escaping the summer heat of Qum. It takes some time before the letters get to me in Damavand.

Let us turn to your question. Our method in understanding the Qur'an is to rely solely on the Qur'an itself. We interpret the equivocal verses with recourse to other Qur'anic verses. Of course, the exegetic *hadith*s that are *mutawatir* or have sufficient truth-indicators are, in our

---

[211] This question was placed by Dr. 'Abd al-Rahman al-Kiyali.

opinion, credible and as such are reliable sources in the enterprise of understanding the Qur'an. For, as expressed by the Qur'an, the sayings and commands of the Prophet are authoritative [*hujjah*] and binding.

The *hadith*s narrated from the *Ahl al-Bayt* possess the same authority as those of the Prophet. Our reason for this is, among others, the prophetic *Hadith al-Thaqalayn*, whose chains of transmission exceed the limit of *tawatur*. We have explained this in the introduction to the first volume of *"Tafsir al- Mizan"*. (In this connection you may also refer to the third volume, where we have spoken thoroughly of the univocal [*muhkam*] and the equivocal [*mutashabih*] verses of the Qur'an.)

But as to the Companions, their Successors, and other authorities of Qur'anic exegesis where they give their independent views, they cannot be relied on—except where their views agree with the *hadith*s related from the Prophet and the *Ahl al-Bayt*. For, their views are conjectures [*ijtihad*] that are, at best, valid for themselves. We consider their conjectures [*ijtihad*] devoid of any value—as is also the case with regard to the unverifiable *hadith*s attributed to the Prophet and the Imams.

We have chosen the aforementioned method of interpretation based on a number of *hadith*s reported from the Prophet and the *Ahl al-Bayt* that explain that the Qur'an is self-sufficient in conveying its meaning. Some examples are as follows. "Indeed the different parts of the Qur'an affirm one another."[212] "The different parts of the Qur'an speak through [the medium of] one another."[213] "The different parts of the Qur'an testify to the meaning of one another."[214] It is the right and appropriate method that has been granted to us by the blessing of the *hadith*s.

---

[212] Ihtijaj vol. 1, p. 389.

[213] Bihar al-Anwar vol. 89, p. 22.

[214] Ibid.

Without doubt, the Qur'an has, like any other work of literature, its peculiar order and structure that render it intelligible. The only instances in the Qur'an that have proven inscrutable to our understanding are the *separate letters*. From this, we may infer that, unlike all the other verses of the Qur'an, the meaning they convey is enigmatic and is not based on the rules of the Arabic language. On the other hand, these letters definitely have a purpose, for the Qur'an affirms that God's word is free of nonsense:

"It is indeed a decisive word and it is not a jest."[215]

Therefore, the insertion of these letters at the beginning of some *surah*s has a purpose. The explanations offered by the Companions, Successors, and other authoritative exegetes regarding these letters are, however, unconvincing.

I have deferred a discussion of these letters to *Surah Ha-Mim-'Ayn-Sin-Qaf* (*Surah al-Shawra*), in the hope that by then God will have unraveled this secret for us—that is of course if death permits. But why did we choose that *Surah*? It is because that *Surah* treats of the nature of Revelation and Divine inspiration and is thus related to the topic in question.

Nonetheless, what has been dawned upon us in regard to these letters up to the present is that there is a peculiar connection between these letters and the content and purpose of the *surah*s they open. For instance, there seems to be a common thread running through the *surah*s that begin with *Alif Lam Mim*. The same holds true in regard to the *surah*s that share, for instance, the opening letters *Alif Lam Ra* or *Ha Mim*. The *surah*s that share common separate letters

---

[215] Surah al-Tariq 86:13-14.

have a discernible similarity in content that does not exist among other *surahs*. An interesting observation in this relation is that *Surah al-A'raf*, beginning with the separate letters *Alif Lam Mim Sad* bears unmistakable similarities in content to both the group of *surahs* beginning with *Alif Lam Mim* and those beginning with *Sad*. This is what we have come to so far; the details are, however, still unclear. We hope that God would unveil for us the truth.[216]

Desecrating the Qur'an

Question

Recently, there has been a trend among publishers in Iran to print certain figures and symbols as spells along with the Qur'an. Furthermore, they attribute amazing qualities to them, claiming that they have been established by the Prophet and the Imams. Are these figures based on authentic Islamic sources?

Do they really bring about the effects that are claimed for them? Let me also ask you about the pictures that are purportedly of the Prophet and the Imams: is it right to print them with the Qur'an (as publishes these days seem to find appealing)?

Answer

Such figures and symbols, whether printed along with the Qur'an or separately, are unfounded and lack religious sanction. The effects claimed for these formulas are either false—as in the case of looking at the "seal of prophethood"—or based on unverifiable sources. Thus,

---

[216] 'Allamah Tabataba'i's reply to Dr. 'Abd al-Rahman al-Kiyali is dated 21 Rabi' al-Awwal 1389 AH.

to print such falsehoods along with the Qur'an is a desecration and a great sin. The same is true of the purported pictures of the Prophet and the Imams.

The fundamental issue here is that the Qur'an is the word of God; it is the central source of Islamic doctrine. It is a living testament to the prophethood of Muhammad, the Divine miracle in which all Muslims take pride. Bearing this in mind, the Muslim believer should never set any other book, though true, on a par with the Qur'an; nothing merits the privilege of being printed with the Qur'an.

This is in relation to writings and books that are true. In regard to such superstitious charts and figures as *muharramnameh, nawruznameh,* or "the rules of *kusuf* [lunar eclipse] and *khusuf* [solar eclipse]" and, even worse, the false and imaginary pictures assumed to be of the Prophet and the Imams, to include these with the Qur'an is to belittle the word of God. Thus, if publishers wish to disseminate books on hagiography and other doctrinal or Qur'anic matters, they should print them separately but then offer them to their customers along with the Qur'an.

Chapter 11: Some Objections and the Answers Thereto

An Objection to the Definition of Islam

Objection

On page four of *"Shi'ah dar Islam"*, the following remark is made: *"Islam* etymologically means surrender and obedience."[217] Though this definition is etymologically correct, in the Islamic culture, *islam* applies exclusively to the religion preached by the Noble Prophet ("That which Muhammad brought").

According to the definition of Islam you offer in that book, we would not be justified in construing Qur'anic verse,

"Should anyone follow a religion other than Islam, it shall

---

[217] Shi'ah dar Islam: 'Allamah's book on Shi'ah history and doctrine. Sayyid Husayn Nasr has translated the work under the title Shi'ah. The quotation here is taken from his translation, p. 46. [trans.]

***never be accepted from him...*"**[218]

to mean that Islam is the ultimate religion, for *islam*, according to your explanation, means obedience, which can take the form of a multiplicity of religions no one of which would be superior to the others. Your definition of *islam* disagrees with *hadith*s that confirm the popular understanding of *islam*. (A number of these *hadith*s is recorded in the second volume of *"Usul al-Kafi"*.) Furthermore, there is universal consensus that *islam* is the name of the particular religion God revealed to Muhammad.[219]

Reply

Let me begin by quoting what I have said in *"Shi'ah dar Islam"*: "Islam etymologically means surrender and obedience. The Holy Qur'an calls the religion which invited men toward this end *"islam"* since its general purpose is the surrender of man to the laws governing the Universe and men, with the result that through this surrender he worships only the One God and obeys only His commands."

Where do I say that *islam* has only one meaning and that is its etymologic meaning or that wherever *islam* appears in the Qur'an or *hadith*s it denotes solely this meaning? What I have said concerns solely the question of appellation and nothing more. You also acknowledge the etymologic meaning of *islam* in your letter: "Islam is absolute submission to God. This, however, does not become manifest unless one utters the two testifications of faith and abides by Islamic rules."

At any rate, *islam* is the name of this sacred religion. This usage of *islam* as the name of a particular religion does not disown its etymologic

---

[218] Surah Al 'Imran 3:85.

[219] This in only a summary of the critic's letter to 'Allamah Tabataba'i.

meaning. As a matter of fact, in Islamic sources, the word is used in both senses. For an example of its usage in its etymologic meaning, it suffices to note the following verse:

> *"And who has a better religion than him who submits [aslama: past participle, from islam] his will to God, being virtuous, and follows the creed of Abraham..."*[220]
>
> This verse indicates that the creed of Abraham was a manifestation of islam in the sense of submission to God. One finds islam used in this sense also in the words of Jacob's children: *"They said, 'We will worship your God, and the God of your fathers, Abraham, Ishmael, and Isaac, the One God, and to Him do we submit.'"*[221]

You further contend that if *islam* denoted the etymologic meaning of the word and not the conventional meaning, we would not be justified in citing verse (3:85) as proof that Islam is the ultimate religion. This contention however is based on two presuppositions: one, that there is no reason other than the verse in question for Islam being the final religion and, two, that in this verse, *islam* denotes the conventional meaning, not the etymologic meaning. Both of these presuppositions, however, are false.

You further write, "*Hadiths* confirm the conventional meaning of the term." No one denies that there is such a meaning. The point is: the conventional meaning does not discard the etymologic meaning. Thus, the *hadiths* in some cases refer to and describe the conventional meaning and in some cases point to the etymologic meaning (i.e., submission, obedience), explicating its various degrees.

---

[220] Surah al-Nisa' 4:125.

[221] Surah al-Baqarah 2:133.

As to your point that people all around the world know islam as the religion brought by Muhammad, there is no question about that. In fact, it was Abraham who first introduced this name:

> *"...the faith of your father, Abraham. He named you Muslims before..."*[222]

Thus, the Qur'an refers to prophets after Abraham and their followers (e.g., Ishmael, Isaac, Jacob, Solomon, Queen of Sheba, Joseph, Jacob's sons, Pharaoh's magicians, and Jesus' disciples) as those who embraced Islam. *Islam* was initially used in reference to the religion ordained by God in allusion to its being submission to Him; it was only in time that it became a proper noun, even as the Divine Names were first used as attributes for God in their etymologic sense, but due to repeated usage over a long period of time they turned into proper nouns for God. Nevertheless, the etymologic sense of *islam* is still preserved, a fact attested to by the *al-* that we occasionally attach to it—*al-islam*.[223]

Shaykhiyyah and Karimkhaniyyah: Deniers of Corporeal Resurrection

Obection

The Shaykhiyyah and the Karimkhaniyyah, two Shi'ah groups, differ from the majority Shi'ah in that they deny the doctrine of corporeal

---

[222] Surah al-Hajj 22:78.

[223] Lit., "the Submission." In the Arabic language, an al- is occasionally affixed to a proper noun that originally was not a proper noun. The function that al- plays in such cases is referred to as talmih or allusion; for, it enables the word to allude to the original meaning of the word while also functioning as a proper noun. [trans.]

resurrection—a principle article of faith—and hold certain unorthodox views concerning Imam al-Zaman. You, however, claim that their differences are not such that would constitute a division from the majority Shi'ah, arguing that their difference lies in certain theoretic discussions not in the rejection of a principle of faith. This argument seems invalid in view of their rejection of the doctrine of corporeal resurrection.

Reply

Division within a religion or denomination occurs when a group of adherents renounce one or more of the primary doctrines of the faith. Now, the two groups in question retain belief in the doctrine of resurrection—which is a primary doctrine of faith—but interpret it differently. One who studies the Qur'an and the *hadith*s and concludes that the resurrection espoused by Islam is an incorporeal one will obviously reject the corporeal understanding of the doctrine of resurrection.

He is not however denying a primary doctrine, for according to his understanding, belief in resurrection, not corporeal resurrection, is an article of faith. That most people understand the doctrine of resurrection to indicate a corporeal resurrection does not make corporeal resurrection a primary doctrine for those who think otherwise. Some may counter by saying that the consensus among all Muslims that resurrection is corporeal makes this belief a primary doctrine. They should however be reminded that assuming that such a consensus does exist, it does not make this belief a primary doctrine, for consensus is authoritative only when it concerns the practical rules of Islam, not theological doctrines.

The Legitimacy of 'Irfan and Tasawwuf

Objection

In *"Shi'ah dar Islam"* where you explain the history and development of *'irfan* and *tasawwuf*, you clearly approve of these two tendencies. (The Imams and the *fuqaha'*, however, have declared such tendencies heretical, and as such they lack any credibility.) You write:

The gnostic is the one who worships God through knowledge and because of love for Him, not in hope of reward or fear of punishment... Every revealed religion and even those that appear in the form of idol-worship have certain followers who march upon the path of gnosis. The polytheistic religions and Judaism, Christianity, Zoroastrianism and Islam all have believers who are gnostics. (132-3)

Your words imply that there are polytheists who worship God out of love for Him. But how can this be right?

Reply

In writing *"Shi'ah dar Islam"*, our intention was to elucidate the Shi'ah doctrine, the history of its development, and its various branches and their beliefs. In accordance with this purpose, we disinterestedly gave some explanation as to the history and development of *'irfan*, without granting them any special credit. We explained reasons, both doctrinal and rational, for their point of view. The purpose of the book was of course not judgmental, thus we did not engage in distinguishing the truths in their claims from falsehoods, and it was for this reason that we did not give a detailed account of the opposition of the *fuqaha'* to them.

As to our explanation that some polytheists are *'arif* (gnostic), we refer to the Brahmins. They undergo severe spiritual exercises to worship the gods. They believe that through these exercises they achieve union, first, with the deities and, afterwards, with God. As a detailed account of their beliefs is beyond the scope of one or two letters, I suggest you study the Farsi translations of parts of the Vedas and the Upanishads, *"Furugh Khawar", "Tahqiq ma li al-Hind"*, and Abu Rayhan's *"Athar al-Baqiyah"* in order to understand Hindu, Buddhist, and Sabean gnostacism.

You further claim that I vindicate 'irfan and Sufism. Yes, I do approve of 'irfan but not that which is prevalent among some Sunni Sufi circles (and which has penetrated into some Shi'ah groups as well) who preach libertinism, play music, and dance. We mean the 'irfan that derives from the Qur'an and the Sunnah, which is based on sincerity in obedience and respects all religious rules. (This latter form of 'irfan we have elucidated in *"Tafsir al-Mizan"*.

A question on the will of angels

Objection

In volume 17 of *"Tafsir al-Mizan"* you write, "They [i.e., angels] do not disobey God in what He commands them. Thus, they do not possess an independent self with an independent will...." This argument seems fallacious. That they do not disobey God does not imply that they lack an independent self. The prophets and the Imams are infallible nevertheless they do possess an independent self and will.

If you mean that they cannot will other than what God wills, that is a universal law that governs all creatures:

"But you do not wish unless it is wished by God..."[224]

---

[224] Surah al-Insan 76:30.

A couple of paragraphs down you paradoxically state that they are capable of perfection. How can they perfect themselves when they lack an independent identity?

Reply

Below that line you quote, we have clarified what we mean by "independent self." We mean the illusion of an independent identity that most people have. When this illusion is erased, egoism vanishes:

> *"They do not venture to speak ahead of Him, and they act by His command."*[225]

Thus, this independent self is what is commonly referred to as *al-nafs al-ammarah*, of which the prophets and the Imams are also free. As to your question regarding their perfection, you have misunderstood my words. The phrase *"min sha'niha al-istikmal al-tadriji"* ("gradual perfection is of its qualities") describes physical matter not angels. In fact, we explain that angels are created in the most perfect state possible for them and so cannot perfect themselves.

Pharaoh, "The Possessor of Stakes" [Dhu Al-Awtad]

Objection

In volume 17 of *"Tafsir al-Mizan"* you mention that some have claimed that the Qur'an refers to Pharaoh as the "Possessor of Stakes" because he

---

[225] Surah al-Anbiya' 21:27.

would impale the criminals with stakes. You discredit this explanation on the grounds that it is not supported by authentic sources. But how do you make this claim when Fayd Kashani in his *"Tafsir al-Safi"* has narrated a *hadith* that confirms this account?

Reply

The *hadith* you allude to is an *al-khabar al-wahid* (i.e., a *hadith* with, at best, a few chains of transmission). In the science of *usul al-fiqh* it is demonstrated that *hadiths* that fall into the category of *al-khabar al-wahid* are useful only in relation to *ahkam* (Islamic rules) and not *mawdu'at* (the application of the rules)—though their chain of transmission be firmly valid [*sahih a'la'i*]—unless they possess certain truth-indicators that definitively affirms their authenticity (such as if we heard a *hadith* directly from the Imam).

Therefore, we cannot employ *hadiths* such as the one in question for interpreting the Qur'an. Moreover, it is a matter of fact, considering the numerous *hadiths* that express the necessity of evaluating *hadiths* by examining their compatibility with the Qur'an that it would be circular reasoning to interpret the Qur'an based on *hadiths* such as the one in question. So, in considering *hadiths* that are *al-khabar al-wahid*, our intention should be to evaluate their coherence with the Qur'an, not to interpret the Qur'an in accordance with them.

Objection

The phrase

> **"...For those who do good in this world there will be a good reward..."**

occurs in *Surah al-Nahl* (16:30) and *Surah al-Zumar* (39:10). Although in both *surahs* the phrase is exactly the same, you take *"hasanah"* in *Surah al-Nahl* to mean reward in the Hereafter and the *"hasanah"* in *Surah al-Zumar* to encompass rewards both of this world and of the Hereafter. On what basis do you make this distinction?

Reply

Despite the similarity of expression, the context in which the phrase appears is different in each *surah*. In *Surah al-Nahl*, the phrase is uttered by God and is followed by

> *"...the abode of the Hereafter is better".*

In *Surah al-Zumar*, on the other hand, the phrase is uttered by the Prophet and is followed by :

> *"Indeed the patient will be paid in full their ajr (reward)."*

In the Qur'anic vocabulary, *ajr* applies to both worldly and other-worldly rewards.

A Point Concerning Job's Supplication

Objection

In volume 17 of *"Tafsir al-Mizan"*, you make the following observation regarding the verse

> *"And remember Our servant Job when he called out to his*

Lord..."[226]: "his calling God by saying 'my Lord' is indicative that he called God to fulfill a need of his." What appears in the verse in question is "his Lord" not "my Lord."

Reply

When the verse says that he called on "his Lord," it means that Job said, "my Lord."

The Story of Job and the Conicting Hadiths

Objection

In your examination of the story of Job in volume 17 of *"Tafsir al-Mizan"* you quote certain Judaic *hadith*s. Then, you discredit them by quoting other Judaic *hadith*s, both of which are derived from the Old Testament. What is your purpose in quoting two contradicting groups of *hadith* from the Judaic tradition?

In the science of *usul al-fiqh*, one of the determinants for preferring a *hadith* over another is its being opposed to Sunni viewpoints. The case at issue, however, involves two conicting groups of *hadith* that are both in accordance with Judaic tradition. So, how do you solve this problem?

Reply

As expressed above, my intention in considering *hadith*s is not to interpret the Qur'an based on them; rather, it is to evaluate the *hadith*s based on the Qur'an. And about your final point regarding the *hadith*s'

---

[226] Surah Sad 38:41.

being in accordance with Judaic tradition, it is impertinent. For, the principle you cite from the science of *usul al-fiqh* relates to religious rules of practice, not to other areas.

That is, if there are contradicting rulings regarding a certain action, the one opposed to the Sunni point of view is preferable. The case at issue, however, pertains to Qur'anic hermeneutics not religious law.

A Point Concerning The Qur'anic Phrase Saying, "It is a great prophecy"

"It is a great prophecy..."[227]

Objection

In interpreting this verse in volume 17 of *"Tafsir al-Mizan"* you reject the possibility of the pronoun *huwa* referring to the Day of Judgment. But why should this possibility be unlikely when the verses prior to this one treat of the Day of Judgment, especially since in *Surah al-Naba'* you explain that *al-naba' al-'azim* is the Day of Judgment?

Reply

*It is true that prior to the verse in question the subject is the Day of Judgment, but verse 65 (**"Say, 'I am just a warner...'"**) terminates that topic and begins a new one. This reading is corroborated by the Surah's ending with this verse: **"And you will surely learn its naba' (tidings) in due time;"**[228] which is a reference*

---

[227] Surah Sad 38:67.

[228] Surah Sad 38:88.

to the Qur'an. Of course, let us point out that both the Qur'an and the Day of Judgment are "great tidings" and so there is no contradiction in al-naba' al-'azim *referring to the Qur'an, on one occasion, and to the Day of Judgment, on another.*

www.ingramcontent.com/pod-product-compliance
Lightning Source LLC
Chambersburg PA
CBHW021441070526
44577CB00002B/235